THE LIGHT BEYOND THE TUNNEL

ANDREA MICHELINI

Original title: *La Luce oltre il Tunnel*
Translated by the Author
Copyright © 2023/2024 Andrea Michelini
All Rights Reserved
ISBN Code: 9798882647734
First Italian Edition: January 2023
First English Edition: March 2024

To my wife Dulce, who has always held my hand along the tunnel

INDEX

DISCLAIMER

All necessary precautions have been taken to ensure that the material contained in this volume is as accurate as possible.

However, the reader should be aware that the material provided has no legal, medical, or professional validity.

These are experiences lived by the author over more than twenty-five years, and they represent only a testimony.

Therefore, there is no responsibility for the use that the reader decides to make regarding the book itself.

PROLOGUE

"Oh God, not now! But why? Why me, and why now?"

Rome, Grande Raccordo Anulare.

Inner lane, heading North.

The thoughts, until that moment just hinted at, become insistent, dark, pounding.

The "Trionfale" exit is now behind, so - rationally - there are just two kilometers left to the "Cassia" exit, but the traffic, which until now seemed smooth, slows down inexorably, forming a snake of cars progressively braking, which stops within a few meters.

Right near the tunnel, which under normal circumstances means being close to home: but there, stuck and who knows for how long, the sense of discomfort grows immensely.

Until the temples ache, until the internal temperature seems to freeze.

Yes, it's getting cold. Or maybe not, it's just me with cold hands and feet.

And the forehead is beaded with sweat.

"Lord, is it possible? Once again? Please, at leats tell me why..."

The question gets lost in the unreal silence generated by the mind. There's nothing to do: even prayers in those moments break like waves against a cliff, announcing the arriving storm. My vision blurs, clenched jaws torture the molars, and the much-dreaded "depersonalization/derealization" materializes, almost inhibiting the mechanisms that regulate breathing. A ton of weight settles - immovable - on the chest, and each inhalation/exhalation seems to be the last one.

I convince myself, based on goodness knows what medical knowledge, that I'm about to have a heart attack.

And there's no way to reason: the fixed idea between the eyebrows says that everything is about to end, that there will be no tomorrow.

Or that, alternatively, madness will take over.

Instinct makes me open the door, I feel like leaving the car there, in the middle of the lane, to climb over the guardrail and run away screaming. But I can hardly feel my legs, how could I run?

Then I think about calling 911, or home, but I fear I won't even have time.

"Will they find me here? Will a passing motorist rummage through my pockets to look for an ID? At least someone will be able to make the identification..."

Foolish thoughts, yet they are the only ones I can formulate, while the once-restrained scream turns into tears.

Torrential, but without sadness or pain. As if it were the logical consequence of what happened in those three minutes - which seem like - of forced stop.

*And an energy I didn't know I possessed
makes me start again, until the exit that
doesn't take me home but to Sant'Andrea
Hospital.
I thank God for being able to get there and
the anguish diminishes slightly, at the mere
sight of a white coat.
Instead of an ECG, the attending physician
gives me ten drops of something I don't
know, but that I swallow with an act of
faith.
In a few minutes everything changes: I
realize I'm myself again, managing
movements and thoughts finally my own.
I still have a residue of tears that I consume
in silence, waiting to be discharged.
The diagnosis: "Fortunately it was nothing
serious, just a panic attack. You're very
stressed, you have to seek help from
someone..."
I go back home finally breathing well, but
with a veil of sadness for what happened,*

and above all because I feel that it will come back.

If what I have just written sounds sadly familiar to you, then I invite you to continue reading.

Here you will find a book with two faces: I will tell you episodes of life lived, in which - I am sure - many of you will recognize yourselves. But interspersed with chapters in which I will try to give you advice/information that have been successful for me, improving my life.

I cannot guarantee success for you, but I have wonderful news for all of you: it took me decades, but at the end of the tunnel the light really exists and I found it.

I sincerely hope to be able to show it to you too.

I.
CHOOSE FREEDOM

There is no doubt that - with the stress and hectic pace of today - panic attacks have unfortunately become a daily concern for many people. Tension builds up until it overwhelms us, as we run non-stop like hamsters in a cage, on an endless treadmill. Although terrible, panic attacks are curable today. We should learn to recognize their symptoms early on, to adopt techniques that can help us to get rid of them well and quickly.

You, who are reading, know very well how it feels before, during, and after a panic attack. It takes you by surprise, unexpectedly: your heart starts pounding, a sense of unjustified fear grips you and turns into real terror.

You feel like fainting, dying, or going crazy. Or all three things together.

Although they seem eternal, panic attacks typically last from ten to thirty minutes.

Not longer: also because physiologically our unconscious defense mechanism that triggers the panic alarm cannot sustain it any longer. A significant percentage of the world's population admits to having had at least a couple of anxiety attacks in their lifetime. But for about ten percent (approximately) of us, these sporadic and transient episodes evolve into the pathology we know well.

Before manifesting full-blown panic attacks, this ten percent of the world's population, however, goes through preliminary and intermediate stages, also common to many other people who - fortunately for them - will not develop a panic disorder. These are all those affected by stress disorders, and, in a subsequent step, by anxiety (generalized or not). For them, the percentage rises significantly, but it can be comforting to know that if these warning signs (stress and anxiety) are not underestimated and, above all, if they are promptly treated, the most serious consequences can be avoided.

It is widely believed that females are more likely than males to experience episodes of acute anxiety or even panic. This statistically proven data is influenced, however, by the fact that many men mistakenly interpret panic attacks as a heart problem; therefore, it is reasonable to deduce that the percentages could be much closer together.

And that therefore no one can think of benefiting from genetic or gender immunity. In the most severe cases, we know that panic episodes can occur daily and even several times a day, proving to be truly disabling for those who suffer from them. They can paralyze us and prevent us from carrying out the simplest daily activities. Moreover, this condition strongly affects the closest family members, even leading to the breakup of a relationship.

II.
PHYSICAL SIGNALS

The power of the mind over us humans goes beyond our common knowledge. A panic attack is certainly one of the best demonstrations of this truth: thoughts not only influence our moods, but even manage to impose themselves on our bodies to the point of determining reactions (or non-reactions) that seem inconceivable to us, in moments of calm or in non-pathological situations. In fact, who among normal people would say that there are moments when we are unable to control agitation to the point of starting to run around screaming or throwing ourselves on the ground? Or, on the contrary, of totally freezing, unable to utter a word, with clenched jaws?

Our mind knows very well how to cause an incredible number of physical disturbances. Since each of us is a universe unto ourselves, it is not certain that everyone experiences the same symptoms when a panic attack is imminent. In summary - in an illustrative but not exhaustive manner - we can make a list of the most common signals, promising to address them again and more thoroughly in the following chapters. If you recognize yourself in more than one of the following, and especially if you experience them simultaneously, it is very likely that you are having a panic attack.

* Dizziness/Vertigo: it often starts just like this. Perhaps you're even abstinent, but the feeling is that you've had a bit too much to drink. The environment seems to sway around you. You might hear a buzzing or a kind of ringing in your ears, and the feeling of "dizziness" can be both objective and subjective.

* Severe difficulty in breathing. Swallowing also becomes difficult, as if you have a lump in your throat. The chest is compressed by an

invisible force, forcing you to breathe slowly but with increasing difficulty. You feel like an athlete who has just run an Olympic marathon (without winning it).

* The heart rate accelerates significantly. Your pulse becomes faster and sometimes even irregular, or at least that's what it feels like. You can't calm the palpitations even by sitting down or even lying down, motionless.

* The face may be paler or redder than usual. You feel like you have a fever. Sometimes you may even feel a bit nauseous and/or constipated. But also the opposite, namely an irresistible need to go to the bathroom.

* Anxiety fluctuates: you try to regain control, and the anxiety seems to decrease. Then, suddenly, it rises again. And just as quickly, it seems to decrease again. All this increases your confusion and frustration even more, generating new and increasingly intense

anxiety.

* Terrible thoughts grip you, or at least truly unwanted ones. And you absolutely can't get rid of them. These thoughts range from everyday worries (for which it seems there is no positive solution) to absurd and totally imaginary anxieties, but they make you foresee the worst possible scenarios: real waking nightmares.

* Upset stomach: you may even feel pain at the pylorus, or in a wider area, as after indigestion or poisoning. You may experience episodes of vomiting, uncontrollable aerophagia. The only possible remedy seems to compress the affected area with your hands, or cover it with warm clothing.

* Derealization/depersonalization: it is one of the most common symptoms, that of feeling no longer connected to the surrounding reality. It is a typical escape technique, which

manifests itself when you feel strongly the discrepancy between what you feel and what is actually happening around you. You know very well that it is an illusory sensation, yet you cannot get out of it, as if you were caught in a vortex. On the one hand, your rationality tries to explain everything, but on the other hand, the emotional side wants to take over at all costs. Often succeeding, unfortunately.

* Loss of control. Panic can easily be considered a loss of control. Even your facial expression betrays the experience you are going through, as your mind seems to want to give shape to the most terrifying thoughts. It all takes place inside you, but you are convinced that you are no longer the master of your thoughts, nor of your movements. Your body stiffens, while you succumb to the fear that grips you.

* One last sensation, particularly frequent: many of us mistake a panic attack for a heart

attack. The similarity between the two can be truly impressive. From personal experience, in these cases it is advisable to consult a doctor or cardiologist, also to avoid the reverse mistake (i.e., mistaking a real physical problem for anxiety or panic).

III.
SYMPTOMATOLOGY

Doctors, psychologists, and researchers in general have long been trying to understand what triggers panic episodes. Nowadays, huge strides have certainly been made, but we are still far from being able to unequivocally define - and therefore treat accordingly - all the anxiety-provoking mechanisms or outright panic.

It is certain that if other family members have suffered from it, you also have a good (so to speak) chance of developing the same disorders. But not necessarily due to genetic/hereditary causes: rather, the reason is very often due to similar or even identical dynamics and environmental and relational situations. Naturally, stress plays a big role, and indeed panic (as I'll discuss in another chapter) often occurs during times of great change: getting married, having a child, changing homes or careers, financial

difficulties...
But also due to those changes that are beyond your control, such as the loss of a relative or friend, a marital breakup, or being fired. Especially if there are pre-existing co-factors.

We have already mentioned panic attacks that mimic heart conditions (and vice versa), but these are not the only ones.
Even for the ones that follow, it is good practice to check whether we are dealing with a physical problem or "just" a psychological one.

• Tachycardia. A tachycardia attack is essentially an increase in heart rate.
This could be a sign of another cardiac condition and the doctor will most likely recommend an ECG to rule out any irregularities.

• Hyperthyroidism. This phenomenon is often accompanied by loss of appetite and weight loss. But fortunately, in most cases, it is curable and can be detected with a simple blood test. An overactive thyroid causes hyperthyroidism.

• Hypoglycaemia. Extremely low blood sugar levels could destabilize your body as it struggles to safeguard and keep your brain functioning. But it could also be a sign of diabetes.
A glucose tolerance test could help determine if this is your problem.

• Excessive use of stimulants. Anything that artificially increases heart rate, such as too much coffee and energy drinks, illicit substances like cocaine or the use of amphetamines, could lead to displaying some of the same symptoms.

• Medication change. If you have taken a certain medication for a long time and then stop, the brain may have an unwanted physical reaction as it adapts to different chemicals.

<u>Always</u> consult a doctor before discontinuing medication: they can certainly advise you on the best course of action to minimize or eliminate any reaction to the change.

• Feeling empty and exhausted can be due to stress, or it may signal adrenal insufficiency, which sometimes leads to episodes of excessive anxiety and panic.
Adrenal insufficiency (inadequate production of cortisol and aldosterone) is a growing concern in today's frenetic world and, if left untreated, can lead to serious consequences.

• Panic attacks can also be triggered by depression. This (as mentioned in another chapter) also explains the success with certain antidepressants, to contain or overcome panic attacks.
It is essential to consider the entire spectrum

of sensations and symptoms. Although it is possible to modify your behavior, it is also crucial to treat yourself with appropriate medication when necessary, and always **<u>under strict medical supervision</u>**.

1996

For someone like me, who has always followed sports (any sport, even the European billiards final between Sweden and Turkey, at two in the morning on TNT Sports), 1996 - which was indeed an "Olympic" year - presented itself as a year truly "to be lived": in addition to the prospect of a comfortable summer in an armchair to watch the Atlanta event in the wee hours, there were nevertheless some significant novelties. At work, I had a very rewarding assignment, I was moving home and, scheduled for the end of the year or thereabouts, we had also planned to get married after some years of happy cohabitation. In short, on the threshold of 35, I felt I was overall a happy man. Not rich, not completely fulfilled, but certainly residing in the half of the world reserved for the "fortunate", those with few but fundamental certainties, to put it that way.

In Rome, it is known, spring often arrives early: and that year, already in early March, it was pleasant to book the field for a five-a-side soccer game with friends, followed by pizza... for recovery, right after. For reasons unknown to most, the ritual invariably took place on Tuesday or Thursday evenings. An understanding and complicit life partner did let me go, and often joined the group and waited for me sitting in the stands, along with other wives or girlfriends. One of those evenings, for reasons I don't recall, I didn't go. I'll be honest, the score didn't suffer much (I've always been easily replaceable on the field), but the news I received made me jump: a dear friend and colleague had a heart attack on the field. Same age as me, apparently in perfect physical condition, trained just enough to feel invulnerable, and yet that evening he remained lying - I was told - motionless for some endless minutes. Lucky coincidence had it that "my" team was playing against another team formed by doctors, among whom were two excellent cardiologists. Like in a thriller movie with a happy ending, my friend/colleague was rescued, taken to the hospital, and saved. Sure, he was done with futsal, but in almost no time he continued to live his life almost as before.

Thoughts began to race through my head: I suddenly realized that certain things happen to everyone, that no one is immune from the "caresses" of fate, and I wondered what would have happened against opponents who were lawyers or engineers, or what could have happened to me too... In short, the trailer of a movie I never wanted to see, but which sooner or later could also come out. Meanwhile, life and work were going well, until one day a colleague - this time much older and a heavy smoker - passed away right in the office, with no warning or symptoms, and due to a heart attack. The matter, beyond the social and emotional aspects (he was a person I highly respected and was friends with), made me decide to undergo every possible and imaginable cardiac examination. I consulted experts upon experts, underwent tests halfway between those of NASA and those of the Olympic Team, always with the same verdict: "You are as healthy as a fish, don't worry". It's easy to be worry-free: but what if they were wrong? What if there was a hidden flaw? After all, my soccer buddy was doing just fine. In a nutshell: I entered that spiral called hypochondria, and began to become one of Carlo Verdone's characters. But mine wasn't a movie.

Since misfortune always sees us very well, even at work things took an unpleasant turn: in less than two months, I lost my job for not wanting to indulge characters who intended to gain advantages at the expense of the company (it happens, it happens...) and so the wedding project also suffered a sudden stop. It was already summer and -

as if that weren't enough - even one of my most solid certainties began to crack: my mother, a person of exceptional strength, became seriously ill. In addition, there was the straw that broke the camel's back: the sudden departure of a childhood friend, who left behind his wife and three young children overnight. The day of his funeral, I was truly devastated: I returned home in the evening and went to sleep, or rather that was the intention. At midnight, something happened that changed my life: I woke up red-faced, drenched in sweat, and with the feeling that I no longer had legs. I went out into the street in slippers, started the car, and drove to the nearest hospital, San Pietro: it was the first time I experienced a panic attack, which in my mind was definitely a heart attack, 101%. It was that night that I first encountered the anxiolytic in drops, that I felt overwhelmed by a series of emotions that would have been enough to give meaning to an entire lifetime. I didn't know it yet, but I had entered a perverse tunnel that would condition my life for the next 25 years. Time and eras are marked with reference to precise events: in ancient times with "ab Urbe condita" and today with "Before Christ" and "After Christ". Personally, I can clearly divide the time of my life between "before that evening" and "after that evening".

V.
STRESS

There are people, those with great responsibilities (such as entrepreneurs, politicians, stock traders), who are generally more prone to panic attacks. But nobody, absolutely nobody, can consider themselves immune, regardless of their occupation. Under strong and constant pressure, tension builds up and eventually becomes full-blown stress. Just like those whistling kettles that emit steam and noise when they reach the right temperature.

Due to a well-known physical law, increasing pressure and temperature, at constant volume (our body and psyche are not expandable), can generate devastating effects: namely, they can literally make us "explode".

The more we subject our body and mind to stress, the closer we get to the dangerously boiling point.

Luckily, we have an extremely intelligent brain. It constantly checks and rechecks its archive to ensure that we have all the reactions and chemicals we need to live our lives.

It's always ready to initiate our flight or fight response.

In less-than-ideal circumstances (those of individuals suffering from anxiety and panic), we can't distinguish – as we'll explain in a subsequent chapter – a real hungry tiger from a... painted one, so instinctively and ancestrally we'll consider them both equally dangerous.

The panic episode is therefore simply our body trying to take care of us, in the same way it did (if it did) when facing a real tiger. And if this – presumably – has never happened to us, ancestral conditioning informs us of the magnitude of the impending (false) danger.

But the fact that our brain believes something is dangerous doesn't necessarily mean it is, quite the opposite. It simply implies that the most basic and primitive part of our body, the one that operates entirely within the realm of instinct (rather than logic or reason), has determined that we need a reaction, even if exaggerated.

This could be since we are constantly on the stress rollercoaster, or because something in our environment has reminded us of something we identify as danger and the need for a fight or flight response.

Let's make a practical example: if you've ever accidentally brushed against a car alarm, barely touching it and it went on, you can understand well how easy it is to trigger something sensitive. Our fight or flight reaction is very similar: we can become so sensitive that we flare up at the slightest event, and it's often practically impossible to stop once the shouts against danger begin.

But the solution – at least in these cases – is simple and it's called prevention. Going back to our whistling kettle, the simplest approach is to prevent it from boiling by reducing the heat and avoiding pressure build-up. Similarly, we can manage and prevent these panic episodes: all we must do is lower the heat. Even if daily stress persists, we can learn to manage it by learning to "unplug" before irreparable damage occurs.

But what is stress?
In simple and essential words, stress is a mechanism capable of disrupting our mental peace, stirring up our emotions.
If not managed properly, it can truly cause serious damage to our minds and our physical health.
Stress makes us feel like we're carrying a heavy burden on our shoulders, causing feelings of anxiety and frustration.

We feel overwhelmed in doing anything, so we start to worry excessively about things we can't control (or don't know how to).

Even small things, those of everyday life, can make us tense and stressed.

There are various things and events that can cause stress.

But what causes stress in one person might not have the same effect on another.

Stress can be physical and internal, or emotional and external.

It can be triggered by a loss we have suffered, by too much work, by illnesses, arguments, and dozens of other issues.

There's also the so-called *office stress*.

Let's be clear: it should never happen, simply because it's not something we should be involved in too much (unless we're the CEO of the company ourselves).

It doesn't do us good mentally, especially if we're dealing with other personal problems.

The dynamics of a job or office can be "brutal", and we absolutely need to know how to handle them.

But the last thing we should do is bring them home with us.

Another common cause of stress is the lack of financial resources. You or your partner might sometimes disagree about finances and budgeting.

For example, you like to save, while your partner likes to spend.

However, your spouse likes to spend because the money is there.

They might care less about saving money for when they really need it. You, on the other hand, are much more careful about this aspect (or vice versa): and the interaction often ends in a verbal argument.

This doesn't solve anything, for either party: it only serves to increase stress, which is exactly the consequence we want to avoid.

Wealthy people, on the other hand, often have the opposite problem: taking care of their money.

Superficially, we might be inclined to define Uncle Scrooge's "stress" (the famous comic book character), always obsessed with the fear of losing his huge wealth, as pleasant: it's instead just the other side of the same problem.

Sometimes we might feel stressed by the effort to make everyone like us (and at all costs). This is especially true for the type of person who doesn't want anyone to be angry with them; therefore, they work to make everyone happy. However, this can stress them out because – while they're striving to make others happy – they have no time for themselves.

And that can be very frustrating.

If we have children, they might feel stressed by the pressure to study hard to keep their grades high.

There are parents who are obsessed with the idea that their children should all receive the highest grades and constantly "haunt" them, as if they weren't entitled to a life outside school.

Often, however, we are the only ones to blame for the stress that grips us.

We get absorbed by worries that go well beyond the normal level.

Or we worry about trivial and useless things. This way, we facilitate stress, especially when we constantly complain and murmur.

Self-pity, at first, may seem comforting. It may make us think that – after all – if things go wrong, it's never our fault.

And this is probably one of the biggest mistakes we can make. We think of negative things, considering them hopeless.

And, in doing so, we accumulate tension. Ancient schools of thought, religion, popular wisdom, are there to testify to this: we attract what we think, be it good or bad.

In Buddhism, one of the fundamental pillars teaches that "we become what we think."

Not to mention the so-called "law of attraction" (excellently treated in the volumes of "The Secret", but not only there), which warns us to change the horizon of our eyes if what we have in front of us is not to our liking or doesn't make us feel good.

The desire to elicit compassion may initially bring some small advantages, perhaps leveraging the solidarity of others, but it's just small "alms" of body and soul.

Much better would do a mature and courageous self-awareness, a review of bad habits, and a resolute change of direction: it would be the best way to scare stress and force it to redirect its energies elsewhere.

Summarizing (without claiming to be exhaustive), here's what can commonly cause stress:

• End of work or layoff

• Illness

• "Toxic" relationships, separation/divorce

- Legal problems
- Bereavement
- Great concern for others
- Feeling "rejected"
- Pregnancy
- Self-pity

Furthermore, stress can also affect us physically if we don't learn how to deal with it.

Headaches, stomach disturbances, and even diabetes can occur.

For us to remain healthy, the immune system must be healthy and functioning properly.

One of the most common health problems is ulcers. Ulcers can affect what we eat, which can cause weight gain or loss.

But other issues may arise as well:

- Back pain
- Neck pain
- Muscle pain
- High blood pressure
- Chest pains

There are also some easily recognizable
danger signs.
A very common one is related to our appetite:
we may either have much more hunger or
none.
We start feeling tired and anxious, as if we're
drained, and with the feeling of not having
had enough rest.
We worry about all those problems we feel we
can't control, constantly asking ourselves,
"how will this end?"
Body muscles (especially joints) are often
sore, and/or we experience long-lasting
migraines. The weaker ones — or simply
those less prepared — may start to
overindulge in alcohol, or even with
dangerous illicit substances.
As soon as we realize these things are
affecting us, we should seek help (family,
medical, psychological) as soon as possible.
Some people who suffer from stress for too
long may reach the point of considering it

normal, like smoking a cigarette: a sort of resignation that amounts to defeat.

And then, enduring long-term stress is not good for health. It leads to problems with the cardiovascular system and high blood pressure.

We may also experience frequent mood swings, especially when we start to realize we've allowed stress to condition us for a long time.

And often we feel no more desire to do what we used to do.

Or simply we don't feel like being with anybody around, shutting ourselves in and potentially triggering another dangerous spiral: the depressive one.

The good news is that there are excellent solutions to long-term stress: one thing we can do is change our lifestyle.

If we tend to overeat when stressed, with a little willpower we can reverse the situation and set up a meal plan to eat reasonably, without necessarily forcing ourselves into a strict diet. Similarly, we should strive to overcome any loss of appetite.

But – above all – we should stop focusing on the negative side of things, trying to tackle them positively.

Once these simple changes are made, then we're already on the path to recovery. And, at work, take a break if stress overwhelms us: remember that life and health are immensely more important than the money we earn.

A stress-free life: solutions

Let's clarify this immediately: getting rid of stress is not an easy task, and before doing anything, you must absolutely understand what is causing stress.

Once understood, we can start managing the *triggers*, the factors that trigger crises.

Pay attention to what happens when you "feel" stress.

Various elements may come into play, different stress factors that affect us physically, emotionally, and mentally.

Nevertheless, there are many ways people can learn to fight stress and get rid of it completely.

Here are some suggestions to use in everyday life:

• If there are events or situations that constantly cause us stress, we should do our best to avoid them, as much as possible. If we can't avoid them, then we should try at least to reduce the amount of time we spend in those stressful situations.

• Focus our energy on the positive things in life.

• When we "feel" that stress is coming, learn to control and manage our emotions.

• Above all, learn to control the physical reactions directly related to stress. Some people tend—when under pressure—to react physically: a harmless way for us and others is to use an object (in this case, stress relief rubber balls) to help.

In more severe cases, when one is already on the threshold of more serious pathologies, it may be necessary to take a medication (preferably mild, or natural remedies) to control anger and actions and help reduce stress levels.

When people deal with things they're unsure of, they tend to worry.
They start wondering if what they did or said was the right decision.
Until they get clarity and understanding, they'll feel stressed and tense.
They'll start wondering what could happen if they made the wrong decision, thus triggering a dangerous spiral of negative thoughts.
Let's see some things we can do to counteract those feelings:
• We cannot, nor should we excessively worry about what will happen to us in the future.
By doing so, we neglect what is happening now, which is much more important.
In short, let's not stress ourselves unnecessarily about what may never happen.

But let's limit ourselves, as much as possible, to living *hic et nunc* (here and now).

• It's not good to worry about what others do. We have no power; we cannot change how they behave or what they do. It's them, those who must live with the decisions they made. And even less can we control others to adapt them to our lifestyle.

Let's accept their decisions and always wish them the best.

Exercise is also an extremely effective way to get rid of stress. We should do it at least three times a week, starting from 20-30 minutes a day: it helps us relax and keep our minds away from what causes stress.

• Start with easy exercises, like a simple walk. Gradually add days and minutes of practice. This is one of the best (and easiest) ways to release stress and keep it away.

• We can also do yoga, jogging, and cycling. For the more adventurous types, rock climbing or mountaineering.

These practices can help relieve stress.

• If we're "angry" about something: boxing, rugby, or martial arts are a great way to release that anger. The anger will move elsewhere and, inside, we'll feel better.
• Basketball, volleyball, and soccer help relieve stress: if we enjoy a sport, while practicing it we feel less fatigue, making our efforts more effective.
• We can take an abdominal ball and use it in the abdominal area. This exercise ball can help us work on our muscles and tone the body.

In general, any type of exercise will help us not only release stress but also keep us in shape.

Eat well

Did you know that stress levels can be influenced by food? Unfortunately, some people don't pay attention to food control and what they eat.

Let's have a look at some of the ways food can influence/help your stress level:

• It's important to follow a balanced and healthy diet to be stress-free. You should try to stick to the number of meals, especially the three basic ones. Never overeat, but above all, never eat only once a day.

• Have light snacks between meals. For example, with apples, celery, and carrots. Skipping a meal is never a good idea. The food you eat should contain many vitamins and nutrients. Breakfast should be one of the most important meals of the day.

• Eat plenty of fruit to control your stress level. Fruit contains a lot of vitamin C and antioxidants. Antioxidants fight free radicals that can contribute to increased stress.

• If you like them and are not allergic, almonds can help relieve stress. They contain a lot of vitamin E and help prevent stress.

• Drinking milk can alleviate stress, as it's rich in antioxidants. Having a cup or two every day is a good way to effectively alleviate stress levels.

• Also, try eating asparagus: they contain a good dose of antioxidants. Another stress-relieving fruit is blueberries, which also benefit eyesight: always keep them handy.

If you believe your stress level is high, it's important to change your diet as soon as possible. The sooner you do it, the sooner you can effectively address lowering stress levels and ultimately getting rid of it altogether.

Other health problems

Stress can greatly influence overall health: depending on how it's managed, it can have positive or negative outcomes. The faster you work to relieve stress, the faster your health will improve.

• Make sure to focus on your health: it's important. Make sure, above all, to eat the right foods, and in the right amounts.

• If you drink alcohol or use illicit substances, this will increase your stress level. Many people, mistakenly, think they're stress-relievers, while addictions can cause serious health damage.

If you feel you're developing an addiction and can't stop by yourself, seek help from medical professionals.

• If you're someone who gets angry easily, then high stress levels can be triggered. Constant anger and frustration can cause hypertension and other health problems. You should work not to let things, especially the most trivial ones, condition you beyond necessity.

Relaxation Techniques

Trying out some relaxation techniques helps alleviate stress and put the mind at ease. Here are some examples to implement in your daily routine:

• Gentle, soft music can be therapeutic for a stressed mind. Just sitting or lying down listening to music can help eliminate the pressures you regularly face. Some good music, especially instrumental, is a great remedy for stress.

• Besides being used as a psychophysical or religious exercise, yoga can also be used as a relaxation technique for stress. Since yoga has no strict concepts, it can work to help you be patient and learn more about yourself. You'll feel mentally fit, as well as physically well.

• Meditation is a great way to deal with stress. For it to be effective, you must focus and maintain concentration. It may be difficult at first, but meditation can really help you get rid of negative feelings, like anger. The more you meditate, the faster stress disappears.

• Try to take a walk in nature, if you can: if there's a trail near you, go through it in the morning or at sunset and admire the scenery.

• Relaxing muscles is another way to relieve stress: when you're stressed, your muscles tense up. Focus and try not to be tense. One way to do this is to sit in a quiet place and close your eyes. Mentally relax the muscles of your feet, then work your way up and relax the rest of your body's muscles. Take some deep breaths and focus on what you're doing, counting each exhalation. This technique should be performed for at least ten minutes.

• Get into the habit of smiling. It takes more effort to frown than to smile.

• Always maintain good posture. Take some breaths and sit up straight. Your feet should be flat on the floor. The lower back should always be slightly bent (backwards, not forwards!).

• Relax your shoulders: keep standing like this for a few minutes and try not to slouch. Stand up straight and maintain posture.

• If possible, find a quiet place and read a good book.

• Express your feelings openly: reaffirm your affection every day to the people you love. Tell them how much you appreciate them.

This will do "miracles," both for you and for
them.

• Prayer, whether you believe it or not,
changes things. People can learn to pray
every day. Pray—even in a secular form—for
things to change for the better in your life.
But don't do it for just one or two days,
assuming that things will change overnight.
It takes months, even years.
You must keep doing it until you see results.
Even after, keep "praying" for other things
that have caused you stress and frustration.

Try to incorporate these "remedies" into your
everyday life. They are very easy to put into
practice and will simplify your life.
However, in the following chapters, we will
delve much deeper into these topics.

Laughter

You should always add a bit of humor to your
life. You can't be serious all the time... You
have to laugh sometimes! Laughter is a good

medicine for you, and you should prescribe it to yourself as much as possible.

Stressed? A laugh will bury it.

When you laugh, repressed anger and frustration melt away like snow in the sun.

In addition to laughing, smile more often too. If you're not used to it, start now: did you know that a smile can be contagious?

Learn to spread your serenity and joy to others who need it. Not only will it help them, but it will also help you.

Mind Control

You must instruct your mind and teach it to alleviate stress. Take control of your mind so that you can be wiser and more constructive. Don't allow your mind to experience feelings of anger and frustration that can lead to stressful situations. When you divert your mind from these, you will be able to focus on other things that do not cause stress.

Always control your mind, learn to take charge of your emotions associated with stress and stressful situations.

You must be able to focus on not thinking about things that contribute to stress.

It will take time, but the more you are able to focus, the more you will be able to cope with stressful situations.

Also, learn to block negative emotions.

If you don't, you'll allow them to take over and you'll end up right back where you started.

Seek out positive thoughts to overshadow the negative ones and the stress: you should be able to understand which thoughts are good for you and which are not.

Don't let negative thoughts or worries pervade your mind and make you feel stressed.

Having control over your mind is a formidable weapon, probably the most important and effective one.

Get Away from Everything

Everyone should be able to take a break from their daily routine.

At least once a year, you should take a vacation away from everything and everyone, even if only for a few days.

The best way to take a vacation is to get away from the "usual" environment.

Even if the destination is only a few hours away, it can help you take your mind off work and stressful activities.

Relaxation and rest will do you good.

Try to go to a different place every time, look for a place that is unfamiliar to you.

If you've never been to a Natural Park, you should go: they are quiet places where you can spend time walking and enjoying the scenery.

Take your family away from the hustle and bustle of daily life. Even if it's for a few days, take them to a place where you all will have fun. If the weather is nice, take them to the beach: kids enjoy playing in the sand, and adults love lying in the sun and enjoying the beautiful weather.

Also, do some shopping – why not? Find a place (but away from home) where you can go just to admire the shop windows. There are many large shopping malls that will satisfy your fantasy.

In short, taking a break and going on vacation is a great method to free yourself from stress. Not only will it help you, but it will also help your family.

But... what about at work?

Sure, we all must face many obstacles at work. There are several things that can stress us out:

• Not meeting a project deadline

• Ongoing disputes with colleagues or the "boss"

• Having a tight work schedule with minimal breaks

However, there are various things you can do

to get rid of stress: for example, adopt a different approach to your work and duties.

Don't think of it as thankless work.

Be enthusiastic about what you do.

Approach the challenge of completing the work positively.

When you adopt a different approach to the situation, you won't feel stressed and forced to do something you don't want to.

Don't leave your desk cluttered with papers and other things scattered everywhere.

Everything should be clean, and you should be able to find everything you need.

This will make the work easier, and you won't feel frustrated every time you need to find something.

Finding yourself in a toxic work environment can really cause a lot of stress.

People who don't get along can ruin the work environment.

Often, employees bring their personal problems to the office.

Or, when they see that you're different in not lashing out at everyone, they'll attack you: since they're unhappy, they want you to be unhappy too. Keep calm, even when you want to retaliate. Retaliating only increases stress levels.

Be kind and, if possible, minimize conversation.

Time Management

Time management is a big issue to deal with, at least for most people. People have become so busy in everyday life that they don't realize how important it is to manage their time effectively. There are some things in our lives that are put on the back burner when they should be put first, instead.

Much of the stress we face comes from improper time management.

To get rid of stress, it is therefore important to learn to prioritize and manage time effectively. There are some things that can certainly be postponed to another day or time.

Here are some ways you can work to rid yourself of stress, learning to manage your time wisely:

• Learn to organize your time with an action plan. Write down activities for the week in a planner. Arrange them in order of importance. Estimate how much time you think each one will take.

• Once the first week is planned, you can start planning future weeks as well. Of course, there is a chance that you won't be able to do everything you set out to do: it's not a problem if, every now and then, you have to adapt to circumstances.

• When managing time in your daily routine, you need to do it wisely. There may be times in your schedule when you have free time. This too can be used effectively and produce results.

• Another way to use your time is to always complete tasks according to schedule. This will alleviate the stress of having to chase after them to complete them.

• Remember that procrastinating not only costs you time, but it also costs you money: it's not healthy and it causes unnecessary stress. It is very important that you manage your time wisely to avoid it becoming a negative habit.

• Keeping organized at home or at work can help you use your time more efficiently. You don't have to waste time looking for things unnecessarily. When things are organized, it doesn't take much to find them when you need them. You can cause excessive stress simply by being disorganized. And you'll end up spending more time looking for what you need than you should.

• Almost everyone has a goal they would like to see realized. However, not everyone succeeds: this is why you might feel stressed, because what you wanted to happen didn't happen.

But always make sure your goals are reasonable, not unrealistic utopias.

• Falling into a comfort zone can be a bad habit.

It can also be difficult to break, if you're not careful. Many times, it's fear that keeps us from moving forward. Many people do the same things – in the same way – for many years and never try to change. There are times when you should find the motivation to make changes and avoid the stress of "repetition". But remember that you won't always have someone around you, encouraging you to do it.

It's important that you take the first step to remove the fear and learn how to do things differently.

• Once time has passed, you can't get it back. Nowadays, time has become a precious commodity: you'll need to set aside time to do things for yourself.

Learn to relax. Turn off the computer, phones, and everything else you're used to having around you. You can accumulate stress simply by not recognizing that you need a break.

• Don't try to do more activities than you can handle. It may not be easy, but it's the best thing to do to avoid excess stress.

At Home

When you're at home, you need a place of your own to relax.

If you have a room in your house that you don't regularly use, turn it into a relaxation room. Design it to feel serene and welcoming. Add plants, paintings, and posters that can create a pleasant atmosphere. Wicker or natural wood furniture is a good choice.

Also, add some cushions, so that you can feel comfortable when sitting or lying down.

Use Natural Remedies to Relieve Stress

Another way to rid yourself of stress is to use herbal remedies.

They usually shouldn't cause any side effects. They are a simple way to get rid of stress, but many people don't use them. These remedies come from natural herbs that work like medicines: of course, they shouldn't be a substitute for medicine, but in this case, they can do a lot for your stress.

There are several types of herbal teas that can help relieve stress, such as:

• Ginger

• Peppermint

• Lemon

• Lemongrass

• Celery seeds

• Juniper

• Chamomile

• Ginseng

Herbal teas not only help you relax and relieve stress, but also help alleviate coughs and flu.

For anxiety, you can use herbs like hawthorn berries and lime blossom. If you suffer from digestive problems, chamomile and peppermint can help you a lot. While ginseng also helps keep colds at bay. But if you're not familiar with these herbs, consult your doctor before taking them.

Other Solutions for Stress

• Get used to not arguing. Never. For any reason. You'd only increase stress levels and blood pressure. In addition, you don't really know what the other person is thinking: it's better to avoid.

• Don't unload your frustrations on someone else just because you're stressed. Take a walk and get away from the atmosphere that's causing you stress.

Learn to Say "No"

If everyone appreciates you, but you feel that something is not right inside you, try to change. The more you try to please people, the more they want (and demand).

The more they want, the more frustrated and stressed you will become.

You can't do everything for everyone. You can't be everywhere others want you to be. You're not "the lamb that takes away the sins of the world," so don't overdo it with your instinct to always make yourself useful.

There are many people who don't mind exploiting you for their benefit, and who don't care about your feelings or your health. So, even if it's easier to say yes for peace's sake, it's better to say no.

Saying no to some requests doesn't mark you as selfish: some might think so, but you have your own personal life. When you learn to refuse some requests, you can devote time to things that are really important to you.

In the past, there may have been things you wanted to do but couldn't because you kept postponing them, meeting the needs of others: am I right?

And, in fact, now that others have gotten used to hearing you always say yes, it becomes much harder for you to say "no".
So, it's good to start saying "no" at the start of the game.
Still, be polite when letting people know that you can't meet their requests. Some of them will try to make you feel guilty: you can't do much about that, just say goodbye and move on your way.
This only shows that they wanted to use you only when they needed something. In the end, they'll get over it. And even if they don't, it's their problem, not yours.

In conclusion, dealing with stress is not easy for anyone. However, you can't allow stress to control your life. Otherwise, you'll end up with health problems and confused feelings. Remember that everyone handles stress differently. Some know how to get rid of it, others don't care to solve it, and still others passively accept being stressed for the rest of their lives.

Stress can be used as a motivator to get rid of your problems, as well as of stress itself.

Using some of the techniques listed before can help you live a better life.

If you look at it from a positive perspective, you'll be able to face stress by continuing to move forward in your life.

Keep living a lifestyle by eating well and healthily.

Also, make sure to include regular exercise in your daily routine: these two things should really be a priority.

If you have a toxic relationship that's been the same for a while, it's time to turn the page: toxic relationships aren't healthy for anyone. They can bring you more stress than you can imagine.

You have to work hard to eliminate stress. It won't happen overnight. But you must do it, day after day.

TRACY

*An evening in June, in Rome, is the ideal
time to start a love story.
Everyone, without exception, has fallen in
love at least once with the help of the
"Ponentino" breeze and the youthful
enthusiasm of those who imagine their
future filled with warm sunny days.
I couldn't miss this call: and she appeared on
the sidewalk of the pizzeria where we were
eating at an outdoor table, enjoying the
pleasant wind of the evening.
Two languid hazel eyes, and those colors of
hers -halfway between auburn and blonde-
struck me mercilessly. I noticed that she was
staring at me intently, so I made an
instinctive gesture, extending my hand: she
ran towards me quickly, wagging her tail,
asking for caresses with her gaze. She must
have been just a few weeks old, they told me
they found her in the countryside around
Benevento while she was rummaging
through the garbage, literally starving.*

With the irresistible charm of a Golden Retriever, expertly mixed with the cunning of a Spitz, she already knew she had conquered me.

After all - the guys she arrived with told me - she was desperately looking for an owner.

The pizza was finished, the bill paid, and I opened the door of my car: with a leap, without even waiting for an invitation, she took her place and crouched down in front of the passenger seat, patiently waiting.

Whoever said that we choose our pets, our four-legged friends? In my case, it was she who chose, without giving me a chance to reply.

That's how it started, in a way that was really unusual for me at the time, a wonderful story of animal humanity (or human animality, it's the same).

Anyone who has had an animal friend knows what I'm talking about.

The others don't, and I'm really sorry for them.

From that moment on, we practically began to live in symbiosis, since I was now working – just a little - mostly from home: my anxieties and panic attacks were daily appointments, almost hourly, experienced with a ritual as repetitive as it was painful. Shortness of breath, tremors, immediate recourse to benzodiazepines in drops, and the urgent need to lie down on the bed or the couch, at the mercy of that haunting storm. Tracy (I baptized her that) soon began to understand, with her strong instinct, the nature of my drama: she stood by my side, motionless, licking my hand that hung from the bed.

She would stay there for as long as necessary, even for hours, looking at me intensely, as if she wanted to say "Be strong, I'm here, I'll help you get through it."

No, mine weren't the thoughts of an unbalanced person: once again, anyone who has had a dog or a cat or any other animal knows well that I'm telling the pure truth.

We communicated with our eyes, and they were loving and intense conversations.

In those moments, I was the "puppy" for her, I was the helpless one she had to take care of. Then, once the storm had passed, we would "celebrate" on the lawn near the house, rolling the ball but actually chasing a moment of normalcy, of mental peace.

If I'm different today, if the shadows have dissipated and if I've truly crossed that tunnel to the end, don't think it silly or childish or who knows what else if I say that it's also thanks to Tracy that I'm writing these lines, hoping to help you too.

Our animals have much shorter lives than we do, and she dedicated hers to me, practically.

I will never forget her.

V.
ANXIETY

What is anxiety?

Anxiety is your body's response to real or perceived threats.

When your breathing rate increases, when your heart beats faster and harder, when you feel "butterflies in your stomach" (and not for romantic reasons) and it seems like you're experiencing strong bursts of energy... then you're probably feeling anxious.

Let's clarify right away: everyone - absolutely everyone - sometimes feels anxious. And a certain level of anxiety is normal - and even helpful - in some situations. Anxiety is the primitive and simplest way your body keeps you safe. A banal example: imagine coming home on foot after a tiring day of work, almost "dragging" your feet and legs from exhaustion. Out of the corner of your eye, you see a dog growling at you and about to attack: well, magically you forget the tiredness and the distance between you and home, and a boost of energy helps you get out of trouble. Anxiety is also a source of positive motivation. Another example: if you have to face an exam or a job interview, anxiety helps motivate you to study or prepare for the meeting. However, experiencing too much anxiety about something or feeling anxiety that is not connected to an important challenge is not helpful. It can really hinder your daily activities and affect the quality of your life.

If you're wondering what the real cause of anxiety is, unfortunately, there's no one-size-fits-all answer. Common causes of anxiety can nevertheless be summarized as follows:

- Not getting enough sleep
- Not taking good care of yourself, including exercising, eating healthily, and doing things we enjoy
- Consuming too much caffeine, such as coffee, tea, or energy drinks

- Meeting new people or attending social gatherings
- It may stem from a period of stress due to financial uncertainties or job instability
- Work, school, or family relationship pressures
- Conflict in romantic relationships
- An unhealthy and "disordered" home environment
- A series of unavoidable commitments
- Serious and stressful events, such as the death of a friend or a family member's illness

And we'll stop here, although we could go on almost indefinitely.

But what are - essentially - the signs and symptoms of anxiety?

People who suffer from anxiety, which we prefer to call "anxiety disorder" (since a certain level of anxiety, *per se*, is not necessarily a problem), show a variety of different signs and symptoms. And different types of anxiety disorders can also have different symptoms.

We list some here, which are the most common ones:

•	Accelerated heartbeat (palpitations) and/or tightness in the chest or throat
•	Rapid breathing or shortness of breath
•	Feeling tense, restless, charged to the breaking point
•	Hot flashes and chills
•	Cold sweating
•	Tremors
•	Nausea
•	Headaches
•	Unjustified weakness and/or fatigue
•	Stomach or digestive problems

Scaling up in grade and intensity, we could have:
•	Obsessive thoughts, excessive worries and fears

- Sense of panic or imminent danger, imagining the worst-case scenario
- Difficulty thinking about anything other than our worries
- Difficulty concentrating and performing daily activities
- Difficulty to fall asleep or sleeping at all

However, always keep in mind that some people may have different symptoms. Our list was intended to be indicative, but certainly not exhaustive. You can use it as a rough guide, **but remember that only a professional can diagnose an anxiety disorder.**

And what is this anxiety disorder?
An anxiety disorder - broadly speaking - can take on pathological levels when anxiety begins to affect a person's life and prevents them from interacting with friends, family, work, or school. Instead of feeling anxious in response to a real danger (the "assault" of the

dog a few lines ago), those with an anxiety disorder will experience the same symptoms in situations they perceive as dangerous (such as meeting new people or taking public transportation).

But anxiety is not just one thing: saying "anxiety" is like saying "headache" or "stomach-ache."

Different pathologies can be associated with the same symptom, although within the same "family" of disorders.

These, from experience, are the most common types of anxiety (but there are others as well):

•	Generalized anxiety disorder: excessive worry about anything, including the... worry of worrying

•	Social anxiety disorder: anxiety in social situations, often rooted in the fear of doing something wrong and being judged by others

•	Panic disorder (which we will discuss in detail in the next chapter): repeated panic

attacks and worry about future, possible
panic attacks
•	Fear of having a panic attack in certain
situations and not being able to escape or get
help
•	Obsessive-compulsive disorder:
anxious thoughts leading to obsessive
behaviors and compulsions to do certain
things
•	Specific phobias: intense fear of objects
or situations

Up to this point, we've covered the causes
and symptoms, but the human psyche is
much more complex and not merely the
result of chemical and physical reactions,
however complex they may be.
There's always more when anxiety becomes a
problem.
Anxiety disorders are almost never - in fact -
caused by a single factor, but rather by a
combination of things, which may include
some of the following ones.

Family history: there is ample evidence showing that people with anxious parents may be more susceptible to anxiety. This is partly due to genetic factors and partly to social learning.

Personality and learned traits: people with certain personality traits may have a higher likelihood of experiencing anxiety. For example, being a perfectionist or shy, or having low self-esteem, can contribute to developing anxiety.

Physical health: some chronic physical conditions - such as asthma, food allergies, epilepsy, diabetes, or heart disease - can contribute to causing symptoms of anxiety.

It's extremely important, even crucial, to understand what triggers anxiety, i.e., things that set off anxiety. Identifying *triggers* is essential if we want to learn to combat it.

These triggers vary from person to person, as we've seen before. They also vary depending on the type of anxiety being experienced. However, there are some common triggers, such as:

- Excessive use of social media
- Caffeine
- Fatigue
- Drug abuse
- Negative thoughts

We didn't mention social media by chance. Among the novelties of recent years, there's a dangerous phenomenon, that of comparison anxiety, triggered by impossible comparisons spurred by certain media phenomena.

And that's exactly what we want to talk about in the following paragraphs.

You might notice that after using social media, you feel more anxious about your life. It can also make you feel depressed or disconnected.

Healthcare professionals and writers often describe anxiety as "a rocking chair, on which you're always moving, but never making progress."

And the worst part is that those around us, our friends, relatives, or colleagues, seem not to notice.

Or - worse yet - they think they're "helping," but in a wrong way.

How many times have we heard: "Come on, you can do it!" while the anxious person can't "do it", simply because they can't control anxiety rationally, as it acts on an unconscious level. Much, much better would be if the interlocutor of an anxious person said to them: "I'm here, I'm listening to you," showing empathy and offering a psychological foothold.

A person who suffers from anxiety experiences situations, that are normal for others, in a very poor way.

In these cases, the most common mistake is to let slip the phrase: "Can you really not do such a simple thing?"

No, they can't. Not because it's not easy, but because of their own situation.

No one would think, talking to a person without limbs, to say to them: "Can't you open the door?"

Anxiety may not be as evident as a physical disability, but it shares the same practical consequences.

Anxious people often seem boring or pedantic because they seek reassurance about everything: "Are we sure it won't hurt me? What do you think, will I make it? Will you help me if I struggle?"

These phrases, which to many evoke sympathetic smiles, are instead vital for an anxious person. The right way to respond is to reassure them calmly and gently (even if it's the thousandth time it's happened) that those who suffer are not alone, and those who care about them are ready to stand by them.

Comparison Anxiety

Comparison anxiety occurs when one constantly compares oneself to others, but with a negative approach.

Typically, one tends to think that everyone else is better off than oneself. And this can lead to developing severe forms of anxiety and/or depression.

Often, we compare ourselves with those who have (or we think they have) a better appearance than us or who are more successful than us.

And when we feel "inadequate," besides morbid jealousy, the sense of inadequacy can be unleashed, in the face of which we often feel powerless. Over time, the effects of this condition can have a significant impact on mental health, and lead to depression.

Many people remain involved in a constant comparison cycle. The question is: are some people more prone to comparison anxiety than others?

The simple answer is: there are still no unequivocal and secure data.

But the wiser one suggests that there are likely some individuals who are more prone to it than others.

Young people aged 19 to 32 have shown to be particularly vulnerable to comparison anxiety. This is not surprising given that when you're younger, you generally seek more acceptance. As they try to find their place in the world around them, young people naturally compare themselves to others.

Furthermore, among these, those who already suffer from mental health problems such as depression are more likely to develop the condition. This also affects heavily those who suffer from low self-esteem.

Comparison anxiety tends to affect women

more than men. Although more men than ever are nowadays admitting to suffering from mental health problems, comparison anxiety tends to be more present in women, at least statistically.

The signs of comparison anxiety are practically the same as any anxiety disorder. However, there are some specific signs of the condition that need to be paid close attention to. These include:

• Feeling depressed or down after using social media

• Being excessively critical of oneself

• Wishing to be someone else

• Dissociation: feeling "unintegrated" rather than "fragmented," with memories, thoughts, emotions, and behaviors experienced as 'strange' and not in line with one's characteristics

• Excessive and obsessive thoughts

• Worrying (too much) about what others think.

These are just some of the main indicative signs of comparison anxiety. The condition causes the same type of symptoms as other anxiety disorders, only one is more focused on others, constantly comparing one's life to theirs.

Anxiety (we already know it well) tends to manifest itself in different ways. When dealing with comparison anxiety, we might experience some specific physical symptoms. These include:

- Heavy and fast breathing
- Sweating
- Lack of energy
- Stomach-aches and headaches
- Hair loss

The physical signs of comparison anxiety tend to develop over time. Hair loss tends to occur when one is overly stressed. So, this would be a symptom for those suffering from severe comparison anxiety.

In addition to mental and physical signs, we'll
likely also notice a change in behavior.
And we may start making choices based on
what others are doing. In fact, when we see
certain successful people, we may feel
compelled to try to follow their path to
achieve the same success.

The problem is that following someone else's
path can never make us happy.
Furthermore, who guarantees the results,
even if we follow others' paths by the book?

Many people suffering from comparison
anxiety also tend to withdraw socially. Over
time, the condition can make us feel "less
than", forcing us to feel uncomfortable in
social situations. And when we begin to avoid
other people, feelings of loneliness and
failure can arise.

As with any type of anxiety, comparison anxiety - if not properly treated - over time can turn into severe depression.
That's why seeking treatment, when there's still time, is important.

Comparison anxiety is a new type of anxiety. Therefore, there is very little specific information to find online. The above are some of the main signs to help identify if you are dealing with this condition. If you are, don't be afraid to seek help from competent people.

Is it the fault of the digital age?
It is interesting to note that the issue of comparison anxiety has only recently been addressed. It's something that has become more widespread during the digital age. So, is the blame on the Internet and social media? They certainly haven't helped, but the condition has existed for decades.

Unfortunately, the Internet makes it much easier for us to compare ourselves to others. So, for those who are already vulnerable to developing comparison anxiety, social media - just to give a banal example - doesn't help at all.

Social media has made it easy for us to compare ourselves to others: we are constantly bombarded with positive posts. For example, it could be a friend who always posts about how amazing their life is. Or it could be moms who post photos of their perfect families (remember the old *Barilla* advertisement? That's the one).
But social media isn't a true representation of real life and success. Just because people post good things doesn't mean there aren't problems behind the scenes. People tend to only post the good things. So, in essence, you're really seeing their highlights, rather than their real life. If you keep this in mind,

you can avoid comparing yourself to unrealistic images of success.

Today, social media is truly one of the main factors behind comparison anxiety. When they were first introduced, around 2006, no one could predict the huge impact that social media would have on our lives. From the rise of the *selfie* to constant updates about our lives, social media has become deeply ingrained in society.
The problem is that people tend to only post the highlights of their lives; rarely, if ever, do they show the bad days. This can create an unhealthy image that everyone else is doing better than us.

And it's not just the *status* posts that are published that can contribute to comparison anxiety: even the use of filters on photos has a negative impact on mental health. Not only are social media great for staying in touch with friends and family, but they also give us exclusive access to our favorite celebrities. There are also tons of online influencers, known for their good looks and successful lifestyles.

When we're overwhelmed with "perfect" images, that's when we can really fuel comparison anxiety.

A group of people who particularly feel the pressures of social media are moms. There tends to be an unspoken, unadmitted competition that takes place on social media among parents. Inputs that push moms (but often also dads) to do things differently, or to compare their children with others: the pressure to be a 'perfect parent' can lead to severe comparison anxiety.

When you struggle to get your children to behave a certain way and then you see pictures of other people's children who seem... angelic, that's when the feeling of being an incapable parent can creep in.

However, the thing to remember is that what you see on social media isn't necessarily real. That perfect family photo that was uploaded might not tell the whole story.
That's why it's important to learn to "humanize" social media users.
This way we'll be less likely to find ourselves "idolizing" the protagonists of certain posts, or the ever-too-often criticized *influencers*.

Sometimes we become jealous of the work and/or wealth of friends we meet online. However, if we were to know and look at their overall situation, we would probably see that they have problems just like everyone else. Remembering that they too are just people, with their own problems, can really help. These are the main ways in which social media contribute to comparison anxiety. If you find yourself comparing yourself to others on sites like Facebook and Instagram, it's time to start using them less and changing your mindset.

It's important to recognize any vulnerability to the effects of comparison anxiety: this way you can seek timely ways to combat the problem before it becomes "too" serious. Living with comparison anxiety can be extremely difficult, forcing those affected to withdraw into themselves and change their usual behaviors.

However, there are things you can do to mitigate its impact, like limiting social media use.

Although it's certainly possible to fight comparison anxiety on your own, in some cases it may be necessary to seek help from an expert. It depends on the severity of the condition and how it's affecting everyday life.

But when, how, and where to seek help from an expert? Below we try to list some of the main signs to look out for, indicating when it's time to seek help.

The easiest way to understand if you need help (or not) is to assess how much and how the anxiety is affecting your life: does it interfere with your daily activities? If so, we may really need help, small or large, to address and fight the problem.

A certain level of anxiety is normal in life, as we already know, but it's when it starts to take over the daily routine that it becomes a problem.
In severe cases, comparison anxiety can affect relationships, reduce work performance, and lead to depression.

The biggest problem with anxiety is that it often creates physical symptoms, as well as mental ones. If anxiety is constant, it can lead to stomach aches, headaches, accelerated heart rate, and even difficulty breathing. If it becomes severe, you may experience panic attacks.

These physical symptoms are often harmless,
but they can have a devastating impact on
your well-being. They can also worsen over
time and pose a health risk if left untreated.
So, even if it's just for the physical side of the
condition, you should seek help if the
symptoms are too difficult to deal with.

A common - and incorrect - way that people
use to deal with anxiety is by avoiding
potentially anxiety-inducing situations.
In the case of comparison anxiety, this
becomes a true "social anxiety", with all the
consequences that follow.

If you find yourself having to avoid certain
situations, it means you're not living with
serenity.
With the help of an expert, you can learn to
fight the "avoidance techniques" that have
developed and that are preventing you from
living well.

Finally, a good sign that you need help is if you're struggling to cope. Over time, comparison anxiety can worsen, especially if measures are not taken to address it.

The worse it gets, the more harmful it will be for your mental health.

It can be difficult to ask for help, especially with a condition like comparison anxiety. However, it's important to realize that it's a common condition and that doctors today are much better at helping people with mental illnesses. Never be ashamed to seek the help you need.

But comparison anxiety isn't limited to situations triggered by social media: it can also occur offline, and often in a more serious way.

The workplace is a common place to suffer from comparison anxiety: whether it's comparing your performance to a colleague's or worrying about not being "the weak link" in the team, comparison anxiety at work can affect performance and mental health.

In these cases, it's good to start by reflecting on how you feel: when we think that a colleague's situation is better than ours, we may feel genuine jealousy. Especially in the case of a promotion they got, thus highlighting our dissatisfaction, caused by an unfulfilled desire for recognition or extra financial gain, as we have seen already.
When this happens, it's likely because you're not yet where you want to be, in your career. But you can overcome this stage by thinking about the results you've already achieved, instead.
Too often we focus on the negative, on what's still missing, forgetting, or downplaying the milestones reached.

Try to write a list of results, even the small or very small ones, that you've achieved at work.

Do it over the course of a year, a month, or even just a week.

Start writing down your results as they happen. This will help you feel more positive about yourself at work and minimize how you compare yourself to others.

If you suffer from comparison anxiety because you feel stuck, setting goals can act as a "lighthouse" and motivator.

This can also help turn competition at work into something more positive.

Think about what you want to achieve at work and how you could become happier, thanks to your work. Then, set small, achievable goals to work on. When you achieve these goals, you'll feel more confident and motivated.

Thinking about it, what successful men in the professional field have in common is that they all set their goals and pursue them with perseverance.

In most cases, they are not smarter, "brighter", or luckier people than you, but they are simply more tenacious and consistent.

For younger people: if you really want to tackle comparison anxiety, it can sometimes help to develop friendships with peers, especially at work. This way, you'll start to see them in a much more positive light. They won't be your competitors anymore, but they'll inspire you to do better.

Always try to get to know everyone at work. Also have a simple chat and start expanding your network of contacts: this can have positive effects on confidence and self-esteem, reducing conflicts and reasons for comparison with others. Overall, certainly, comparison anxiety at work can be difficult to deal with. However, the ones seen above appear to us some of the best suggestions to follow. Understanding why we constantly compare ourselves to others can also give us the opportunity to see how we can change such behavior.

Comparison isn't limited to interpersonal relationships; for example, we often find ourselves worrying about our finances. These are also instances of comparison anxiety because it's natural and human to compare our financial situation with that of others.
These concerns are extremely common, but we must carefully try not to lose sight and control of them.
Easy to say, but in practice?
In our daily lives, we can start by observing why we're comparing our financial data with someone else's. Why do they have more money than us, for example? Certainly, if someone has a better lifestyle than ours, it's easy to feel envious.

This is especially true when struggling to overcome a difficult financial situation. Another possible reason is thinking that others, even with similar incomes, might have savings and therefore a more substantial bank account. Regardless, once we understand the discomfort related to comparing our financial situation with others, there are still ways to address it.

You can start, for example, by regularly checking your available funds, between income and savings. Create a budget and look for ways to cut monthly expenses. Then, set a goal to save a certain amount each month for as long as necessary to solve a problem or change a situation.

Do it every month, regularly: with care and close attention, you should see improvements, even if minimal, in a short time.

And in the meantime, learn to recognize things that aren't working and replace them with virtuous behaviors.

Simply taking care of your money, controlling its flow, can be enormously helpful: even if you don't achieve the practical goal, you'll certainly achieve a feeling of control, of being able to cope with problems, significantly alleviating anxiety.

Often, comparison anxiety in economic/financial contexts stems from social conventions that are difficult to eradicate: realizing that we have visible financial problems to many people causes a sense of serious embarrassment and shame. In a society entirely based on appearance and material possessions, a deficient financial situation is experienced with shame, or at least embarrassment.

And it's often a reason for self-accusation: "I've made mistakes that have led me to this," or "If I had behaved differently...", and so on.

And the concern doesn't come so much from "not having/owning" enough but from the fear of being judged. More than the real consequences of a situation, we worry about others' opinions.

And here we must convince ourselves that there's nothing to hide, nothing to be ashamed of.

Everyone makes mistakes and everyone learns from them. Remember that a problem is always an opportunity to improve.

So don't feel 'behind' those who have more, don't feel like a 'failure' just because you haven't yet reached your goal.

Remember that we all have different life paths. And they unfold in different times and ways.

We just have to learn to walk at our own pace: the goal is the destination, not the time it takes to get there.

Another of the most common forms of comparison anxiety concerns body image.

Let's admit it: nowadays, men and women
are under tremendous psychological pressure
to always look their best.
We're constantly being sent images
illustrating how we should appear: perfect
body, flawlessness, boldness, and optimism
at all costs.
But life isn't – and can't be – the cover of a
glossy magazine.
Certainly, promoting a healthy body image is
a positive message, but too often it's
exaggerated to the exact opposite.
For this reason, comparison anxiety is a real
problem today, for millions of people.
But how to stop constantly comparing
ourselves to others?

One of the best ways to fight comparison
anxiety is to tidy up our social media. If there
are particular people who trigger comparison
anxiety, it's best to stop following their posts
for a while (even better, remove them
altogether).

This also applies to all the pages we usually follow: some of them, despite their intentions, don't send positive messages but trigger anxiety.
Cleaning up social media can have a huge impact on our well-being.
And, most likely, we'll discover contents, accounts, and pages that truly inspire us and make us feel good about ourselves.

So, while there are undoubtedly many influencers out there who worsen our comparison anxiety, on the other hand, there are some that focus on the positivity of body, mind, and spirit.
And they can also teach us to become more confident.

It's important to learn to love our body, mind, and condition.
With this, we don't mean to say it's easy, quite the opposite: especially if we've conflicted with ourselves, with our image, or

our character for some time.

But if we truly want to fight comparison anxiety, it's time to start learning to love ourselves: body, mind, and soul.

The first step is to stop – if possible, reset – negative thoughts.

Every time we catch ourselves thinking something negative about our body, we need to change it into something positive.

Some women are ashamed of their body, perhaps not as elastic and slender, since they've had children. Instead of futilely desiring to regain the lost shape, they can focus on the joy of being mothers and having wonderful children who will love them forever, no matter what their physical appearance.

A man with gray hair or perhaps bald, "sculpted" by years and the effort of work, can similarly compensate for what – looking in the mirror – he doesn't like with pride for having built a peaceful life for himself and his family.

Finally, another way to deal with comparison anxiety is to stay active.
When we exercise, endorphins are released, providing a sense of lightness and happiness. They also help increase self-esteem and provide security: so, never forget to include physical exercise among our priorities, if possible.

So far, we've listed some practical tips, useful to follow at least in an initial phase. And if they're not enough, it will obviously be necessary to seek professional help.

Yes, because comparison anxiety can really have a series of negative impacts on our lives. Multiple studies have been conducted exploring the effects of this condition: while some conclusions are clearly obvious (such as depression), others can be truly surprising.

Comparison anxiety can be challenging enough to deal with. However, it can also lead to other consequences on mental health. Untreated, as mentioned earlier, it can lead to depression: because it can cause significant self-esteem issues. The more negatively we compare ourselves to others, the more it influences our mood.
But – in addition to depression – comparison anxiety can also lead to other forms of anxiety. These include generalized anxiety and so-called "social" anxiety.

One of the first warning signs is the difficulty to fall asleep and a tendency to wake up several times during the night.
There may be recurring thoughts that keep us awake or less prone to falling asleep.
Using tablets or smartphones in bed is strongly discouraged, to avoid being too emotionally involved and also because of the

light they emit, which is a frequent cause of insomnia.

When we sleep little and poorly, stress and fatigue increase.

And, consequently, we're more exposed to experiencing anxiety.

We've also said that one of the most common effects of comparison anxiety is the feeling of low self-esteem.

This makes those who suffer from it feel as if they're not worthy of experiencing happiness or aspiring to success.

And, because of the vicious cycles we've unfortunately come to know, other conditions can be experienced, such as depression.

Or, again, they can also have an impact on the life choices we make. Often those who don't feel "worthy" of love cultivate — unconsciously — unhealthy relationships, as if to "punish themselves" for their condition.

In the most severe cases, they detach from the external world. They lose the desire to go out and face people, or it becomes difficult to form or maintain friendships.

Additionally, stress levels increase: the problem is that excessive stress can have a negative impact on virtually every aspect of life. It can increase the incidence and severity of mental health problems, and also cause physical issues.

We know well that overcoming any type of anxiety is not an easy task. However, there are techniques that can be learned, even to overcome comparison anxiety.
While comparing ourselves to others is a natural human behavior, it becomes a problem when experienced in an unhealthy way.
To defeat comparison anxiety, it's important to avoid its triggers, namely anything that can trigger it. For example, by limiting the

use of social media (as extensively described before).

By reducing the opportunities for negative experiences, we can focus on improving our thoughts, and above all, we can work to recognize our weaknesses and strengths.

Indeed, too often when we compare ourselves to others, we tend to focus on weaknesses. At the same time we "hide", more or less consciously, our strengths.

Everyone, without exception, is good and capable at something: it's just a matter of recognizing it and putting it into practice.

So, first of all, let's try to make a list of all our strengths.

And when a feeling of negative comparison overwhelms us, we can mentally go through the list and remember the (many, believe me) positive aspects.

One of the best ways to overcome comparison anxiety (and not only that) is to practice

gratitude. Being grateful for the things you have in your life can prevent you from feeling distressed about what you don't have or what isn't as you would like it to be.
Some studies have shown that keeping a "Gratitude Journal" for just 21 days can significantly change your perspective.
You'll learn to focus on the things you have, rather than on those you don't.

But I promise you that we will return much more extensively to this aspect in the last part of this volume.

These are some of the best ways to overcome comparison anxiety. Although it's natural to compare ourselves to others, this should never take over our lives. If you find that the above suggestions don't work for you, it may be time to consider therapy: it could help you better understand the problem and develop long-term strategies to overcome it.

CURITIBA

Curitiba is a beautiful yet little known city in the Brazilian South-Central region. As the capital of the Paraná State, it's a significant cultural, commercial, and industrial hub. Blessed with a mild climate and populated by numerous descendants of Europeans.
In short, a city where living doesn't involve too much of a cultural shock, as it might elsewhere in the same country.

My wife and I arrived in Curitiba during the southern winter (July or August, I don't exactly recall), attempting to start a new life after the disappointment of a recently failed entrepreneurial venture in the state of São Paulo.
In our suitcase, hopes and illusions occupied almost all the space, as money was truly scarce.
But we seemed rich, or at least well-off, because we were staying on the tenth floor

of a very elegant hotel. For two fundamental reasons: in Brazil, someone with a foreigner's face like me is better off avoiding budget hotels, and especially because at that time the Euro-Real exchange rate was 1 to 7. So, with less than a thousand euros per month, you could feel like a nabob, or close to it.

We met entrepreneurs, presented projects, and even offered ourselves for much less prestigious roles than the ones we aspired to: but the astral conjunction, karma, or whatever you want to call it turned its back on us.
After almost a month, finances had further diminished, but what worried us the most were the prospects: we didn't know whether to return to São Paulo, go even further south, or even return to Europe.

And it was at that point, without even warning signs, that the understandable stress once again overwhelmed me, after having been quite well for a certain period.

One evening, the light in that hotel room seemed to dim, and my ears began to ring annoyingly. I got up from the bed and tried to get some air, but the effort was titanic.

It was perhaps the only time in my life that I found myself on the verge of fainting, and for this reason I laid down on the carpeted floor, my heart pounding.

Suddenly, a sense of terror mixed with helplessness made me emit a terrifying scream, as I tried to tear off my pajama jacket as if it were Hulk's shirt.

I thought I had reached the limit, and with mad lucidity, I rushed to the window, trying to open it to take the final leap.

It was only my wife's love and faith that saved me: I don't know where she found the strength, she so petite compared to me, to grab me by the neck and arms and drag me back to the ground, holding me tight and

*screaming incessantly for me to come back
to myself.*

*I remember those endless minutes perfectly,
as if it all happened yesterday.
And I know, years later, that one can
emerge from this condition.
But it takes more than medication, therapy,
and willpower: Support and Love
(intentionally capitalized) from those who
care about us are also needed.*

*In these lines, I'm not addressing those who
are suffering so much, but those who live
alongside them: you have a wonderful
power in your hands, don't ever get tired of
using it for those you love.
You'll win together.*

VI.

PANIC

We've finally arrived. We're entering the lair of our worst enemy: Panic.

Not that anxiety and stress - as we've seen extensively so far - have been our friends, but when these disturbances evolve into full-blown panic, then we have a serious problem, often even disabling.

But what are panic attacks, really?

Sure, we're familiar with the phrase "panic attack." But at the same time, many of us aren't entirely sure of what they are and what causes them. If, as I believe, you're dealing with an issue related to panic, the good news is that you're certainly not alone, as panic attacks are much more common than people think.

In simple but effective terms, panic attacks are intense and sudden feelings of mixed fear and anxiety. They can occur at any time, even when you think you're relaxed. They tend to last between ten and twenty minutes, but the effects can persist for several hours. While panic attacks can be very unpleasant and lead to emotional complications if they recur frequently, they are not physically dangerous. The physical effects of a panic attack vary from person to person, and from case to case.

Symptoms commonly experienced include chest pain and shortness of breath. These symptoms can easily be mistaken for those of a heart attack, especially if the person is experiencing a panic attack for the first time. Other physical symptoms include fainting, nausea, and hot flashes.

What are the causes of panic attacks?
While there are several factors that can contribute to a panic attack, the exact causes are unknown. Panic attacks can sometimes be triggered by significant changes or

stressful life situations, such as a new job or the loss of a loved one.

Some people with phobias also experience panic attacks when they are exposed to anything they have a phobic aversion to. Having a panic attack in a particular situation can also lead a person to believe that the situation has the potential to trigger another attack. These cases are known as situationally bound panic attacks.

Other factors may be more long-term and make a person more prone to future panic attacks. People who suffer from psychological conditions like anxiety disorders also tend to experience panic attacks.
These recurring long-term cases are known as panic disorder. Panic disorders can affect anyone, but they typically affect young adults and tend to occur more frequently in women than in men. They are usually treated

through psychological therapy, medication, or a combination of the two.

Panic attacks can create confusion and fear, especially while they are occurring. But knowing a little about them is the first step in helping yourself overcome them.

An important tip: hyperventilation can worsen many of the symptoms of a panic attack, while controlled and deep breathing can help alleviate the symptoms.

Panic Attacks or Panic Disorder?

Panic attacks are a sudden feeling of intense and disabling stress or anxiety. A single panic attack is not dangerous, even though it may seem frightening at the time. But what about frequent panic attacks? Could they be a sign of a bigger problem?

Panic Attacks

The physical symptoms of a panic attack are caused by a response from the body's sympathetic nervous system. These symptoms most commonly include chest pain, shortness of breath, hot flashes, and dizziness, among others. They are often mistaken for a heart attack, especially if the person is experiencing their first episode. During a panic attack, the individual may feel as if they are losing control. They may also experience a sense of impending doom or begin to feel detached from themselves or reality.

Often, the reason for the onset of a panic attack is not clear even to the sufferer. Panic attacks like this can be a one-off occurrence or something that happens very rarely. But recurring cases of panic attacks may indicate that the individual has a panic disorder.

Panic Disorders

People who suffer from panic disorders undergo frequent panic attacks. Unlike an occasional acute panic attack, these even more pronounced attacks are often related to situations that have caused problems in the past. Simply fearing another panic attack in a recurring and uncomfortable situation can cause enough anxiety to trigger a panic disorder. It's a vicious cycle that causes many people to completely avoid past situations where they've experienced a series of attacks. Although the exact cause of panic disorders is unknown, they are treatable. Often, they are treated through therapy or with the help of self-help strategies. These therapy sessions are usually sufficient to mitigate the problem, but -in some circumstances- medications must also be used.

Moreover, learning a little more about what it feels like during a panic attack can help you feel relatively more relaxed, even as they occur. Reading a book on anxiety or panic attacks can really help (and that's exactly what we're trying to do here, despite all our limitations).

However, the best course of action is generally to speak with a doctor or mental health professional. They're always the best choice.

Having a single panic attack is not a sign of a panic disorder. But be careful, as untreated panic disorder can lead to a much greater number of panic attacks and perhaps even further complications across the board.

Always remember that if you believe you're suffering from any type of panic disorder, seek help before the problem truly begins to have a negative impact on your life. Technically, we're talking about "Panic Attack Disorder" (PAD) when panic is not limited to a sporadic, episodic case but occurs at regular intervals, as many of our readers surely know.

As always, let's try to define when and how we might suspect that we are affected by Panic Attack Disorder (PAD):

•	Presence of recurrent and unexpected panic attacks, out of the blue.

•	Persistent concern, for at least one month after experiencing a panic attack, about having another one.

•	Worry about the implications or consequences of a panic attack (such as thinking that the panic attack is a sign of an undiagnosed medical problem). For example, some people undergo repeated medical tests due to these concerns and, despite reassurances, still fear falling ill.

•	Significant changes in behavior, related to panic attacks (such as avoiding activities like physical exercise because it increases heart rate).

During a panic attack, one is suddenly overwhelmed by the physical sensations described above. We've mentioned that panic attacks peak in about ten minutes and usually last for a maximum of half an hour, leaving the person tired or exhausted.

They can occur several times a day or only once every few years. They can also occur while people are sleeping, waking them up during the attack. Many people experience a panic attack once or twice in their lives; this is common and is not Panic Attack Disorder (PAD).

But panic attacks are surprisingly common: it is estimated that up to 40% of the population will experience a panic attack at some point in their lives.

Some of the common signs and symptoms of a panic attack include:

- Overwhelming sense of fear/terror
- Thoughts of dying, choking, "losing control," or going crazy
- Increased heart rate

- Difficulty breathing (feeling like there isn't enough air to inhale)
- Excessive sweating
- Dizziness, light-headedness, or feeling faint
- Trembling
- Feeling nauseous and/or stomach pain
- Numbness in limbs or tingling
- Hot or cold flashes
- "Derealization," that strange feeling that oneself and/or the external world are not real

If you experience at least three or four of the above symptoms, it can generally be concluded that you are suffering from Panic Attack Disorder.

The Onset of Panic Attacks

Despite the pressures faced in contemporary society, our bodies do not desire anxiety and stress at all. In short, just like the proverbial

African gazelle that wakes up and must run to escape the lion, when it would rather not.

Our natural protection mechanism is the so-called *fight or flight* response, which is one of our most basic and primal defenses, as well as one of the most powerful. Its purpose is to always be active to protect us from a car brushing past us as we cross the street, from the tile that comes loose from the roof as we pass under a house, from the tree falling near us in the forest: in short, from everything that stands between us and life. This reaction (whether it is flight or fight) accelerates our heart rate and releases adrenaline, with the aim of saving our lives.

The fight or flight reaction is designed to resist and confront the threat, or to escape it. It is a natural occurrence. The problem arises when the alarm signal is misinterpreted, that is when - in the absence of a real danger - we develop such a reaction only because we associate the signal with a danger, albeit non-existent: that is, when we experience the anticipation or prospect of harm that could befall us. We could call it a "conditioned stimulus."

Two examples in this regard are provided by science and common experience: in the first case, we will talk about Pavlov's dog.
The Russian scientist Ivan Pavlov would ring a bell every time he was about to feed his dog. This went on for several days, until one day he rang the bell but did not give the dog any food. Well, the dog started salivating and secreting gastric juices even in the absence of food. This simply because it had learned to associate the sound of the bell with the arrival of food.
The other experiment can be done by any of you who own a cat: get into the habit of shaking the bag of kibble every time you feed it. You will soon notice that - shaking any box containing small objects like pebbles, for

example - your cat will hurry to you, as it had associated the noise of the box with food.

In practice, a neutral stimulus (the bell or the noise of the box) can become a conditioned stimulus (salivation or the cat running towards you).

Our body also works in the same way: a siren makes us think of an ambulance, a police car speeding, or even (where there is a war) an imminent bombing.

The brain urges us to hurry, but in pathological situations our body freezes, unable to react effectively.

When – instead - we are "healthy" (at least physically) adrenaline provides us with the fuel to fight the danger or the speed in our legs to run away.

This is particularly true when we find ourselves - for example - walking down a street where we had an accident years ago, or visiting a hospital where a relative died some time ago. Even in the absence of accidents or hospitalized relatives, our mere presence there can cause us, in order: discomfort, stress, anxiety, panic.

Changing streets or not going to that hospital is generally the most obvious solution, but it is never the ideal one, at least in the long term.

To heal and come out of the tunnel, we must find a way to be stronger than that unpleasant stimulus, or to accept it for what it is. But we'll come back to this later.

Stopping Panic Attacks

Panic attacks are generally described as sudden and extreme attacks of fear and apprehension. Although these attacks can occur at any time, stressful or traumatic situations can make you more likely to experience them. That said, one important thing you can do to help ward off future panic attacks is to learn to manage stress properly. Here are some tips to get you started:

- *Count to ten*

At the first sign of alarm, when a stressful situation arises, step away from the problem and count to ten. Use this time to collect yourself and think about the right decision to make.

- *Practice deep breathing*

Deep or abdominal breathing is how your body naturally breathes when you're relaxed. Deep breathing comes from movement in the abdomen, rather than chest movement that accompanies shallow breathing. When an individual is stressed, they generally tend to take breaths that are too rapid and shallow. This, in turn, increases stress and can easily trigger a panic attack.

- *Pay attention to stress factors*

Make a list of the things in your life that often cause you stress. Then try to develop a plan to address or overcome these situations the next time they arise. Having an action plan will make uncomfortable problems much less stressful to deal with.

- *Start an exercise routine*

Exercising a little every day does a lot to improve your physical and mental health. You don't need to adopt an intense and rigorous routine. Even 30 minutes of walking, jogging, swimming, or a similar activity every day will do you a lot of good. This well-structured routine makes life more in order and controlled, minimizing your stress.

- *Turn to friends*

Panic attacks are very difficult to be dealt with, alone. If you have a friend or family member you trust and can share your feelings with, ask if they're willing to lend you a hand. Having tangible support helps a lot. Just make sure the person you confide in is not connected to the things that generally stress you out. For example, if your colleagues cause you stress, talk to a friend outside of work.

- *Avoid stressful situations*

When you feel that something is causing you stress, every time you find yourself facing it, it's best to do everything you can to avoid the problem. Even if you can't avoid an unpleasant situation forever. You still have to face the issues you've avoided, once you feel up to it.

There's nothing you can do to guarantee that you'll be forever free of panic attacks in the future: but taking control of the stress factors in your life will prevent you from feeling overwhelmed or out of control.

Natural remedies

Before resorting to pharmacological therapies (which can still have side effects, and pretty serious), there are several things you can try to ward off panic attacks naturally. Here are some:

- *Chamomile*

Chamomile contains anxiolytic properties and is commonly consumed as an infusion, like tea. Some of the calming compounds present in chamomile act by binding to receptors in the brain. These same receptors are the ones that respond to drugs like – for example – Xanax and Valium. Chamomile, with its slightly sedative attributes, has been used for centuries as a natural aid. The herb is often included in medical studies related to anxiety. The results are promising, when compared to placebos. Part of the ragweed family, chamomile can also be taken in pill form or as a powder substance.

- *Lavender*

The scent of lavender has been used for centuries to calm nerves and combat anxiety. Like with chamomile, clinical studies indicate that lavender aromatherapy is a non-pharmacological alternative suitable for combating feelings of nervousness. One study revealed that lavender oil was equally or almost as effective as Lorazepam, without the dangerous side effects. It is also considerably less expensive than pharmaceutical products.

- *Vitamin B12*

When the body doesn't receive enough vitamin B12, some people feel more susceptible to panic attacks and depression. Replenishing a B12 deficiency is quite simple: you can use a doctor-prescribed spray. Vitamin B12 is also found in a variety of foods such as grass-fed beef liver, yogurt, shrimps, game, eggs, wild salmon, and lamb.

- *Valerian*

Valerian is a sweet-smelling flowering herb that grows in the summer. It has been used for medicinal purposes since ancient times. Today it is often taken in the form of dietary capsules as a sedative and sleep aid. Valerian is often combined with lemon balm or hops in an attempt to enhance its positive effects.

- *Kava Kava*

Kava Kava is a Polynesian plant commonly used to relieve worries. The roots are processed to create a sedative beverage. This beverage often replaces alcohol as a treatment for social anxiety. Why? The answer is simple: Kava Kava calms but does not impair mental cognition.

- *Omega-3*

Omega-3 dietary supplements are popular as part of almost every routine supplement. Omega-3 have anti-inflammatory properties, which makes them good for heart health. It has also been shown to reduce symptoms of anxiety and depression. So, it's a suitable way to help in the fight against panic attacks.

Now that you know new ways to stop panic attacks naturally, it's time to try them. If one doesn't seem to work, just move on to the next. It won't happen overnight but, with patience, you should start to notice a difference.

Dispelling Worries

Let's face it: panic attacks make us live through real horror movies, but often we think we are the only spectators. This is because "others" seem all healthy, cheerful, smiling...

Sure, on the outside, we may appear in excellent health (yes, even us!), but inside, we have a fire that is devouring us.

That's why we tend to feel alone and unique in some way.

Nothing could be farther from the truth: know that the problem is quite widespread and more common than you might imagine. Many people have suffered from it, and many of them (including myself) have found ways to reduce or completely eliminate panic attacks.

Those who suffer from it believe they know everything or almost everything, but they have many misconceptions about panic attacks. Maybe you have some, too, like the ones that follow:

1. "My heart will stop, and I will die." Regardless of how strong your heart is beating in your chest, it is much more powerful and resilient than you think. It is the strongest muscle in our body and is built to withstand rapid increases, like when playing a basketball game or dancing frantically. Of course, if there is a pre-existing heart problem, it is good to have it tested for your peace of mind, but for most of us, our heart will be perfectly fine during and after a panic attack.

2. "I won't inhale enough oxygen to send to my lungs." During a panic attack, it is difficult to breathe properly, that's true. However, know that you are taking in more

air than you think. Hyperventilation causes tension and subsequent shortness of breath because your breaths generate an excess of oxygen circulating through your body.

3. "I might faint now." No, you won't faint: your body is just trying to protect you from harm. If there were a physical threat, your body would encourage you to stand and move quickly away from danger. Even if your threat is not tangible, your body is increasing the sensitivity of your awareness, and you are extremely vigilant. If the worst happens and you faint, consider the advantages: if you faint, at least you would have some relief from feeling your chest pounding continuously. The feeling of fainting is caused by hyperventilation. Even if you feel weak, your muscles are absorbing oxygen and are prepared and ready to act.

4. "I'm having a stroke." Your body is experiencing a variety of sensations, trying to

figure out what is causing them. But the physical sensations are not the result of a deeper problem, like a stroke. Your body is not about to explode. It is just doing what comes naturally in times of tremendous stress.

5. "I'm going crazy." You don't feel in control, so the whole experience might boil down to feeling like you're losing your mind. Instead, it's your body reacting to the impulse to flee from where you are. And this, if it can console you, is a perfectly reasonable response to your problem.

6. "I've completely lost control by now." No, you are still in charge; it's just that a different part of the brain is working to *fix* your body. And your body is allowing the subconscious to take over, so that your conscious mind can stop worrying about the false alarm that haunts you. Your body is still in good hands, rest assured; it's just in the *hands* of a

different section of your brain.

7. "How embarrassing, I feel embarrassed!"
Even in these circumstances, social
conventions might embarrass you. And panic
attacks are extremely personal experiences.
But what might embarrass one person is not
necessarily what embarrasses another.
Remember that, while you might think
everyone can see how you feel, most of what
you're experiencing is not visible to others.
Most panic episodes last about ten minutes,
and certainly no more than twenty or thirty.
Take a break and go to the bathroom or
pretend to have a private phone call.
Everything will pass and return quickly to
normal, without others noticing.

Drawing on personal experiences and the
success achieved through practice and
perseverance, I advise you to take a
whiteboard, a large sheet of paper, a sticky
note to stick on the refrigerator, and write on

it: "The panic attack will pass because..." and instead of the suspension points, add in pencil one, two, ten, a hundred positive sentences.

Read it and reread it several times a day, especially when you feel good (essential: in moments of tranquillity, our brain is more prone to learning and storing information). This is the first step towards victory against panic attacks.

Helping Others

So far, we have mainly addressed those who suffer from stress, anxiety, and panic.

We tried to offer explanations, advice, and remedies to solve or at least alleviate the suffering of certain moments.

Now let's try to address those who are or feel close to someone who is experiencing problems related to the emotional sphere.

When someone experiences a panic attack, it is usually more frightening for that person to face it alone. An exception might be if the same individual is in panic because they have difficulty being with people.

If that's not the case, and if you find yourself with someone who needs assistance, there are numerous things you can do to help. The following are just a few of the many possibilities.

Keep Them Calm

Having a panic attack can be a very frightening experience. One of the best things you can do for someone who is suffering is to help them stay calm. Look for a simple activity you can do with them; this will give them something to focus on. It can be something easy, like raising their arms or counting to ten. If possible, find something a little more challenging for them: the sense of accomplishment they feel when they finish the task should help them feel more in control.

Take Them to a Quiet Place

Getting through a panic attack means calming down, which can be difficult to do in a noisy or chaotic place. Try to encourage the person to move with you to a calm, quiet place if they are willing. Consider asking them if there is a particular place they would like to move to and help them get there, if possible. However, don't be too forceful about it, as it could potentially make the situation worse.

Help Them Breathe

People experiencing a panic attack tend to hyperventilate, especially if it's the first time they've felt the sensation. Shallow, rapid breaths decrease the amount of carbon dioxide in the bloodstream. This can lead to symptoms like headaches, weakness, dizziness, or tingling in the hands and feet. When people experience these symptoms, they often feel as if they're not getting enough air, which makes them hyperventilate even more. Encourage those who suffer from panic attacks to take slow, deep breaths, doing it yourself to provide an example. Inhale slowly, count to three, then exhale slowly, and repeat. There's a good chance this will have a positive effect on them.

Stay with Them

When someone is having a panic attack, they might feel like they want to be alone. But the best thing you can do for them is to stay and keep them calm. Remind them that you're there to help them. They might say rude or aggressive things, but try to keep in mind that they're confused, perhaps angry, and still not thinking clearly, so they certainly don't really mean what they say.

Take Care of Yourself Too

If the person you're trying to calm down sees that you're starting to panic, things could get worse. It is perfectly normal to feel stressed or have high concern for your friend during this situation. But you must make sure to stay calm and in control; it's the best way to help them.

Of course, these are not the only methods for helping someone who is having a panic attack. Everyone responds to different things. If the first thing doesn't work, try something else. The most important thing to do is to keep trying.

But above all, show empathy, let them know that you are close to them, and – absolutely – never belittle or ridicule their behavior, even if it may seem silly, childish, or irrational.

VII.

AGORAPHOBIA

Anxiety and panic episodes, if not treated properly, can escalate into agoraphobia (from the Greek αγορά = square and φοβία = fear, hence "fear of the square").
This is one of the reasons why it is recommended to seek a therapist (doctor, psychologist, psychiatrist) as soon as possible.

Agoraphobia develops when a person suffering from panic attacks worries about having one in a public place, where they will not be able to hide their symptoms from others. Usually, this is a place from which they cannot readily escape, or where other people will certainly notice their discomfort. It is estimated that about 30% of those who have panic attacks develop agoraphobia sooner or later.

Agoraphobics are mainly afraid of specific things.

If you experience one of the following symptoms, I advise you to consult your doctor as soon as possible to diagnose possible agoraphobia:

•	Being outdoors: when you don't have well-defined physical boundaries, you feel exposed and vulnerable.

•	Going to public places, shopping malls, or being in a crowd: it may seem almost the opposite for an agoraphobic, it feels like everything is "closing in" oppressively and you feel suffocated.

All you want is to get away, and fast.

•	Traveling by plane, bus, and train: here too, you find yourself among the crowd and you don't even have the opportunity to escape.

•	Using an elevator or crossing a bridge: two structures from which it is difficult, if not impossible, to walk away from.

- A bar, cinema, or restaurant from which you cannot leave whenever you want.

- Any strange, unfamiliar, or out-of-the-ordinary area. Many agoraphobics withdraw into themselves, preferring to stay at home where everything is under control.

But people who experience panic episodes can acquire additional phobias or other obsessive-compulsive disorders. These concerns arise when your mind naturally wants to avoid foods, forms of exercise, or behaviors that you believe are triggering your panic episodes. If you are exposed to these triggering factors, it is very likely that you will experience new panic episodes in the future.

VIII.
FOOD, DRINKS, AND PANIC

Even what you eat, drink, or consume in general, can increase the chances of having a panic attack.

There are three substances, in particular, that can negatively affect it.

These are: sugar, alcohol, and caffeine.

They are proven to induce anxiety. Obviously not in a direct way, but they can raise your overall level of concern, which can exacerbate the situation.

Sugar

Many people nowadays use sugar as a quick fix. This causes a massive wave of mood swings when going from low to high sugar levels, and then back low again, like a yo-yo. A sugar addiction problem is generally indicated by a craving for sweet or carbohydrate-rich meals (donuts, cakes, etc.). Lactic acid can build up in the bloodstream due to sugar consumption. A high amount of this could cause a mental state of panic.

Sugary foods also require insulin to counteract their effects in the bloodstream: the body naturally produces (when healthy) a large amount of insulin, which reduces the amount of sugar in blood. This can create agitation and your mood can fluctuate as blood sugar levels rise and fall. If you are prone to panic episodes, a low glycaemic index or low sugar diet is recommended. Since refined carbohydrates quickly convert into sugar, it is advisable to consume natural meals rich in whole grains, vegetables, and proteins.

Alcohol

Alcohol is a powerful stimulant, regardless of your mental condition. Drinking alcohol also increases levels of lactic acid and raises blood sugar levels. Additionally, it makes it difficult to exercise rational judgment or perceive things clearly and objectively.

Caffeine

Caffeine may make you feel energized in the morning, but it can have a negative impact on your ability to manage stress. Caffeine can inhibit the activity of adenosine, a molecule that controls cellular activity in the brain. For example, it is important in the sleep process: caffeine disrupts its ability to initiate the process, increasing neuron activity.

This stimulates your body to produce adrenaline, as it believes there is an imminent emergency.

Increased adrenaline can alter heart rate and put your body in a reactive state: this could cause strong nervousness.

Caffeine also causes the accumulation of lactic acid in the body. If you feel you are consuming too much caffeine from both coffee and caffeinated soft drinks (such as energy drinks and cola), gradually limit the intake to alleviate the problem. Monitor your caffeine consumption from all sources: green tea, which also has many health benefits, contains a lot of caffeine.

If you really can't live without drinks like coffee, tea, and sodas, try switching to decaffeinated to see what happens. It may take time, but in the long run, it's a much healthier option.

Foods that help in case of panic attacks
At first glance, it seems to make little sense to say that some foods actually help reduce anxiety and panic. And yet it is true.

Of course, we cannot expect to eliminate the problem simply by eating and drinking certain things. But there are certainly small adjustments that can help us, even in this aspect.

Fruits and vegetables
Fruits and vegetables in general are a great source of antioxidants. Antioxidants help the

body fend off infections. They also seem to have something to do with mood balance and more effective blood sugar management.

If you don't like eating fruits and vegetables, why not try drinking them?

Smoothies are very popular and undoubtedly a tasty alternative. You can make smoothies with almost any combination of fruits and vegetables, just be a little creative: give it a try!

Probiotics

Probiotics? What are they? Don't worry, you're not the only one who doesn't know them.

Let's say they are substances secreted by the intestine, tiny grains of good bacteria that live in the gut. One of the most popular sources of probiotics is certainly yogurt.

An Irish study revealed that mice fed with probiotics linked to yogurt showed fewer behavioral traits associated with depression, stress, and anxiety.

Fish and poultry

Fish and poultry are essential for any balanced diet. Each of these choices provides a wide variety of nutrients, including vitamin B, zinc, and iron. Fattier fish (such as salmon) are rich in omega-3 fatty acids or "healthy fats".
Healthy fats promote brain functions, and also help alleviate symptoms of depression and anxiety.

Panic attacks, as you well know, are certainly not fun. These episodes of extreme fear can come to life without warning. By adapting your menu and using the suggestions above, you can certainly influence the possibility that anxiety and panic attacks will ruin your day.

IX.
MEDICATIONS, THERAPIES, TREATMENTS

I want to reiterate, at the risk of sounding repetitive, what was written at the beginning of this volume, but that is always good to remember: any and all therapy, especially pharmacological therapy, should always (and I emphasize **always**) be prescribed by a doctor!

DIY treatments are the most dangerous thing that can happen, especially for those suffering from anxiety and/or panic disorders.

That being said, if your panic episodes are frequent enough to interfere with your daily life, you should absolutely seek professional treatment. While many self-help techniques can help you break free from the grip of panic attacks, it is crucial that you receive all the help you can to prevent it from taking over your life. Whatever you are told to take or do, remember that you are still in charge.

Consider the pros and cons of each treatment, and most importantly, if you feel you are benefiting from it.

Many people - always if advised by a doctor - benefit greatly from adopting a variety of treatments to control their panic episodes.

Anxiolytics

They are a category of psychotropic drugs capable of minimizing anxiety and panic disorders, feelings of distress.

Among these, very common are those of a particular group, called *benzodiazepines*, capable of controlling (albeit only temporarily) excessive anxiety and consequently stopping panic attacks.

They obviously have various unpleasant side effects (and precisely for this reason one must strictly limit themselves to the dosage prescribed by their doctor) such as addiction, excessive sedation, physical and psychological dependence.

Antidepressants

Most doctors (but each case is different) currently seem to prescribe antidepressants to those suffering from frequent panic episodes. Although created to treat depression, they do not act only on that; indeed, they have been shown to be quite effective with patients suffering from panic attacks.

Antidepressants work by influencing serotonin levels in the brain. Unlike benzodiazepines mentioned above, however, they are not a quick fix; antidepressants take two to four weeks to start working.

Many people stop taking them after the first week because they believe they are ineffective: in this case, absolutely call your doctor and explain your problem in detail. Different antidepressants are available and determining which one best suits your needs could be difficult. They all have side effects, and it is up to you and your doctor to decide if they are worth taking.

Antidepressants called "SSRIs" are the type generally most recommended for panic attacks, as they are specifically designed to alter serotonin levels. Some patients have also reported that panic symptoms worsen during the first days of using the medication, before subsiding.

If you suffer from panic disorder, you will most likely need to take an antidepressant for at least a year. This is a long procedure that - let's remember - must be carried out under the direct supervision of a doctor, to avoid endangering your health.

Long-term use of the drug is preferred for these people.

If you have undergone cognitive-behavioral therapy while taking antidepressants, panic episodes are less likely to occur after stopping the medication.

Cognitive Behavioral Therapy (CBT)

CBT is the acronym for "Cognitive Behavioral Therapy."

If you want an approach that includes conversation and counseling from a psychologist, it has been shown that this is a beneficial path for over half of people suffering from panic attacks or agoraphobia. This type of therapy works because it seeks to help you analyze why you might have thoughts that lead to a panic attack: it then helps you regulate your behaviors to manage stress accumulation.

The theory behind cognitive therapy is that the way we think causes panic episodes. All harmful and negative thought patterns are recognized, as are all erroneous beliefs or thoughts you may have ("everyone thinks I'm useless," for example). Many of these erroneous ideas could repeat in a cycle before a panic attack; therefore, recognizing and addressing them can sometimes be enough to prevent another attack, or at least reduce its impact.

Cognitive-behavioral therapy provides techniques to help you avoid the avoidance difficulties that are common in cases of panic disorders. The therapist will help you walk through the events that trigger an attack and make you feel more secure and in control, minimizing the likelihood of a panic attack in these situations. This may involve the use of breathing methods, for example.
Often an effective alternative (or at least a valid add-on) to medication, this strategy can really be successful. However, it is crucial to choose an experienced therapist who specializes in panic disorders and be prepared for a long course of therapy. It won't be solved in one or two sessions, especially if the panic disorder is rooted in your daily life.
A mix between antidepressants and therapy is often recommended.

New Treatments

Alongside the treatments listed above, in recent times some alternatives (often proven effective) have been proposed to try to solve stress, anxiety, and panic. Among these, new technologies have provided quite relevant solutions.

Virtual reality

Take, for example, the fear of flying, often a real source of anxiety and panic attacks.

Well, it's certainly not easy, nor cheap, to find a plane that takes you around while you learn to cope with your fears.

But using virtual reality, wearing a headset that shows 3D images of what it's like to be inside an airplane, can be just as effective. When the plane's engine is turned on, specific seats start vibrating, like the real ones. Plus, with headphones, you can listen to the voice of a virtual captain making an announcement. Finally, take-off, with faithfully reproduced noises and the seat moving as in a real simulator, helps little by little to free oneself from anxiety, precisely because you are aware of being in a test environment, safe.

For many, then, subsequently getting on a real plane has translated into a significant decrease in anxiety, thanks to this particular "training," as revealed by a 2019 study published in "Frontiers in Psychology": it was found that those who used virtual reality - along with other therapies - were more likely to complete and maintain treatment compared to those who had never done it before.

A London blogger, who had found cognitive-behavioral therapy ineffective in treating her *cleitrophobia* – or "fear of being trapped" – had refused for years to take the subway. But after the third session of virtual reality (performed in a large tube simulating a tunnel), she was surprised - in her words - by how comfortable she was.

To go "green"

If you talk to a gardener, it is very likely that he will tell you how calm and relaxed he feels after working the soil. Having a "green thumb," therefore, can influence not only simple harvests: "organized gardening," guided by a qualified therapist, is used to treat anxiety, depression, schizophrenia, and post-traumatic stress disorder in hospitals, shelters, community gardens, and correctional facilities worldwide.

A 2010 study in the Journal of Health Psychology found the first evidence that gardening can relieve stress: after just 30 minutes, participants' levels of the stress hormone (cortisol) decreased significantly.

In Lexington, Kentucky, a refuge house has even been set up where around forty patients, mostly women, can work on a 40-acre farm, coming into contact with nature and alleviating symptoms of stress, anxiety, and fears.

Eye Movement Desensitization and Reprocessing, or (EMDR) Therapy
EMDR stands for "Eye Movement Desensitization and Reprocessing." High-sounding terms, for an innovative and - above all - highly effective procedure for anxiety states.

During the sessions, patients discuss targeted traumatic memories while engaging in eye movements as directed by their therapist. Typically, a therapist moves their hand back and forth through the patient's field of vision, and the process seems to alleviate the pain of those memories. It is therefore a matter of "erasing" the emotional torment of painful memories?

No, it's not exactly like that; EMDR does not erase negative memories, but rather "changes the way the brain encodes experiences," according to Deany Laliotis, director of training for the EMDR Institute in Watsonville, California.

EMDR is based on the idea that unprocessed memories of our past, such as sadness over a parent's abandonment of the family, cause us distress and can lead us to react poorly to present problems. When we experience anxiety, our brain is "hijacked" to react to the situation as if it were the same as previous experiences".

EMDR requires patients to confront those scenarios head-on to stop the "hijackings" and reduce negative reactions.

Therapeutic "Chatbots"

Imagine (you can) the perfect therapist: always available, who never judges you, and above all who never presents you with the bill at the end.

It's called a "chatbot," a way to interact with artificial intelligence.

Therapy through artificial intelligence seems to be constantly increasing. Among these is

"Talkspace," where, instead of a human therapist, you send a message to a *bot* that has been programmed by a therapist. Chatbots are trying to fill a gap in mental health: anxiety being a condition that affects about a third of the world's population, therapy with artificial intelligence is certainly an economical and easy-to-use alternative. Of course, it is not a fully approved medical device, it does not claim to cure anxiety, nor can it replace traditional therapy.
But it acts very well as emotional support to help manage anxious feelings.

OLYMPIC STADIUM

During what I now call "my previous life," I was deeply involved in soccer, professionally: primarily as a journalist, then as a scout/agent, and finally also as an executive of a small Brazilian club.

Those were intense decades, during which I had, in a sense, the great fortune of being paid to pursue a passion of mine, one that I had cultivated since childhood.

But, at the same time, this potential "golden age" coincided chronologically with my worst moments in terms of mental health.

Anxiety and panic, as you know, strike when you least expect them, just when everything seems to be going right.

And so it was that on a beautiful spring afternoon in Rome, as I was heading to the Olympic Stadium to do my job, halfway up the final flight of stairs to the Press Stand, my breath was cut off, my vision began to blur, and the cheers of the crowd in my ears first became muffled, then silent and without echo.

Just like that, without any warning, without even that annoying sense of growing anxiety that at least has the merit of acting as a warning signal: none of that, within less than five seconds I had gone from a state of absolute tranquility to real terror.

I seem to remember barely finding the strength to enter a restroom, loosen my tie, and wipe the cold sweat from my brow.

Not far away, I spotted the door to the Emergency Room, which at events where tens of thousands of people gather is always equipped with all emergency equipment and highly qualified medical personnel.

I believe I pushed the door open with force and whispered, with the little voice I had left, that I didn't feel well at all.

I didn't even finish the sentence: two strong and competent arms made me lie down on a cot, while others took my blood pressure and listened to my heartbeat carefully. They even performed an ECG, all within a timeframe of 20 minutes, maybe even less.

With truly commendable promptness, they had ascertained my situation, and soon realized that it was not an emergency at all, but a completely different problem.

The atmosphere became more relaxed, and even I - although the panic attack had not completely subsided - began to feel a bit safer.

Throughout the whole match, and even afterwards, the medic and I (whom I later learned was a highly respected sports doctor) talked about me and my history, my problems and fears.

I received a series of truly valuable advices from him (including a series of tests and exams that I scrupulously underwent the following week), but I was struck above all by his empathy, by the dedication with which he was helping me through that delicate phase, and without even administering any sedatives.

After two hours, I emerged from that experience very tired, but with renewed confidence.

And this, thanks to a doctor who that day had gone far beyond his simple duty but had dedicated himself to helping "the next person" especially on a human level.

I don't have his consent to reveal his name, and I don't even have a contact to trace him, but in these lines I want thank him my own way, with a consideration that I hope will please him: I wish all people suffering from panic attacks to meet, at least once in their lives, a doctor like Dr. A.P.

X.

THE VAGUS NERVE

The vagus nerve is the tenth of twelve pairs of cranial nerves and is the longest in the body. The Latin word "vagus" means "wandering," describing the path of this nerve through the various organs of the body.

The vagus nerve originates from the cranial box, precisely in the spinal cord, and in the neck it branches into two, extending to the abdomen.

The vagus nerve affects the sensitivity of the respiratory mucosa and transmits the rhythm, strength, and frequency of breathing. It affects the pharynx, larynx, esophagus, trachea, and bronchi, as well as the nerve fibers of the heart, stomach, pancreas, and liver.

But it also performs the reverse function: it receives signals from internal organs and sends them to the brain to be processed.

The most interesting aspect for us (and here's why I wanted to talk about this nerve) is the relationship between the vagus nerve and anxiety, as it also transmits signals of nervousness or calmness, anger or relaxation. To understand the link between vagus nerve and anxiety, we need to know that our nervous system is composed of two "opposing" systems that constantly send information to the brain.

The sympathetic nervous system prepares us for action, primarily releasing hormones like adrenaline and cortisol. The parasympathetic nervous system intervenes in rest and relaxation.

In practice, both systems function as an accelerator and a decelerator (or a brake). The sympathetic nervous system accelerates and activates us, while the parasympathetic nervous system helps us relax and slow down; it uses neurotransmitters – such as acetylcholine – that decrease heart rate and blood pressure so that organs may function more slowly.

Functions of the vagus nerve

The vagus nerve controls the parasympathetic system. It intervenes in many functions, from mouth movements to heartbeat.

Some of the functions of the vagus nerve in our body are:

- It helps regulate heartbeat, controls muscle movements, and maintains the rhythm of breathing.

- It maintains the functioning of the digestive tract, allowing the contraction of the muscles of the stomach and intestines to digest food.

- It facilitates relaxation after a stressful situation or indicates that we are in danger and should not let our guard down.

- It sends sensory information to the brain about the state of the organs.

Vagus nerve and anxiety

When we are subjected to stressful situations, the sympathetic nervous system is activated. If tension persists and we cannot deactivate the physiological response that triggers it, it won't be long before problems arise.

The brain responds to stress and anxiety by increasing the production of hormones that travel from the hypothalamus to the pituitary gland, where they induce the release of another hormone, which in turn passes through the bloodstream to the adrenal glands, stimulating cortisol and adrenaline. If the vagus nerve is unable to activate relaxation signals, the sympathetic nervous system remains active, causing the person to respond impulsively and suffer from anxiety.

How to take care of the vagus nerve?

Vagal tone is an internal biological process that represents the activity of the vagus nerve. Increasing vagal tone activates the parasympathetic nervous system, meaning we can relax more quickly after a stressful situation, which will have a positive impact on our emotional balance and overall health.

There are various techniques for stimulating the vagus nerve:

1. Exposure to cold
We know that cold exposure activates the vagus nerve because it stimulates the cholinergic neurons that run through these innervations. In fact, a study conducted at the University of Oulu in Finland found that regular cold exposure helps reduce the fight-or-flight response triggered by the sympathetic nervous system. A 30-second cold shower or a cold towel on the face may suffice. Some people also lie face down and place an ice cube on the back of their neck. Others prefer to quickly drink a glass of cold water.

2. *Diaphragmatic breathing*

Most people breathe air between 10 and 15 times per minute, meaning they have shallow breathing. Ideally, we should breathe in air 6 times per minute. Therefore, another very effective vagal stimulation technique is deep breathing.

Diaphragmatic breathing activates the vagus nerve, and the brain interprets it as a need to calm down, even if the nerve did not specifically give that order. It's the same mechanism by which, if you close your eyes and tap your fingers on your eyelids, you'll perceive brief flashes of light because the brain interprets them that way.

Diaphragmatic breathing involves deeper breaths that bring air into the lower chest, using the diaphragm correctly and promoting relaxation.

3. *Meditation, yoga, and Tai-Chi*

Meditation can increase vagal tone. Researchers at Oregon University found that just five days of meditation activate positive feelings towards oneself, which activate the vagus nerve while modulating the activity of the parasympathetic nervous system.

Practices like yoga and Tai-Chi are also ideal for stimulating the vagus nerve. A study at Boston University revealed that yoga increases neurotransmitters that promote feelings of calmness and serenity, helping to combat anxiety and stress.

Tai-Chi, on the other hand, can balance heart rate, which means it stimulates vagal modulation, according to researchers at the National Yang-Ming University School of Medicine in Taiwan.

XI.

DIS-IDENTIFYING WITH THE EGO

So far, we've explored concepts of physiology, psychology, medicine (albeit at a purely informative level), and first-hand experiences that I'm sure many of you will at least partially relate to.

However, there's a significant limitation: we've viewed the "human machine" simply as the product of the interaction between a physical body and a mind, also physical but capable of producing ideas, thoughts, and sensations.

Now, in the following lines of this chapter, I'll reveal the secret – perhaps the only one truly valid and useful – that can revolutionize your life, triggering a process of definitive and lasting healing.

It's a secret that I personally learned and that allowed me to definitively exit the tunnel, to immerse myself in that light that years before I wasn't even able to glimpse.

Despite Science, Medicine, Psychology, and all followers of Positivism, the true enemy of Man is the mistaken self-identification with one's own body and mind.

Descartes' *"Cogito, ergo sum"* proves flawless only when we take three-dimensional space and linear, monotonous time as reference points.

A bit like the hamster in its cage, for which the world reduces to a spinning wheel on which to run until exhaustion, wrongly believing to be on an endless, straight road with no beginning or end.

Or like the two-dimensional inhabitant of "Flatland" (in Edwin A. Abbott's magnificent tale) who cannot conceive the reality of a sphere coming from "Spaceland," a three-dimensional world: simply, the protagonist sees a point gradually *expanding* into a circle, then sees it narrow back into a point and disappear beyond their – limited – two-dimensional plane.

Academic Science does just that: it observes phenomena and tries to interpret them rationally, using the tools at its disposal.

With the presumption of always having all the necessary knowledge and all the suitable tools to explain any phenomenon.

And without ever humbling itself, like recognizing that "*there are more things in heaven and earth, Horatio, than are dreamt of in your philosophy,*" to paraphrase Shakespeare.

The absolute certainties of doctors, biologists, psychiatrists, and psychologists mean that human actions and reactions are categorized based on physical and mental criteria.

And, as such, they can only be treated "scientifically" through the use of drugs or supportive therapies.

Let's clarify further: relying on professionals in the field is certainly a valid method, and we would never (as widely stated from the first lines of this volume) disrespect such professionals or – worse – denigrate or belittle their work.

Instead, we want to explain that beyond what has been said, there is, in our opinion, an absolutely necessary component that is too often neglected or even ignored: the reality of Man as an expression of something metaphysical.

Man is not just an agglomeration of cells, tissues, organs, and brain electrical impulses. Or rather, not only this.

According to ancient teachings, which over millennia have transformed into religious and spiritual currents and doctrines, at the foundation of everything lies an "Atman."

In Hindu and Buddhist philosophies, Atman is the eternal and unchanging essence of a Human Being. Some describe it as the "soul" or the "true self," but it is in any case the source of all consciousness and individuality.

Long before being formulated by Adi
Shankara, an Indian philosopher who lived in
the eighth century AD, the fundamental
concepts of Advaita Vedanta were already
present in the "Upanishads," sacred texts
written around the ninth century BC.
But what is "Advaita Vedanta" (literally
"Non-Duality")? It is a teaching according to
which the individual self and the ultimate
reality are the same thing.
In other words, the individual self is not a
separate entity from the ultimate reality but
it is rather a manifestation of that reality.
The illusion of separation is caused by the
ego, which creates the sense of "I" and "mine"
and induces people to identify with their
body and mind rather than with the ultimate
reality.
This is because our "ego," the physical and
temporary (in this existence) manifestation
of our immutable essence, cannot go beyond
its own boundaries. Worse still, aware of its
own human and mortal nature, and therefore

subject to the passage of time, diseases, and aging, the ego ends up creating a state of anguish, anxiety, and often even panic, which takes over and causes the sensations we are all too familiar with.

But by realizing the uniqueness of the individual self and the ultimate reality (through meditation and self-inquiry), one can overcome this illusion and realize their true nature as pure consciousness.

Let's try to explain the concept with a simple example: imagine a stormy ocean, moving with large waves.
The ego is the single wave: clearly visible and recognizable when in action, but once it breaks on the rocks, it disappears.
But the wave (which thought itself to be unique and separate from the rest of the sea) was formed from the water itself. The water doesn't disappear but transforms.

The same molecules are no longer seen as the
high wave seen before, but they "live"
immutable and eternal in the same ocean.
Just as those of the waves that preceded it
and those that will follow.

The goal of Advaita Vedanta is to help us
realize that everything is connected and that
we are all part of the same thing. When we
understand this, it can help us feel more
serene and happy.

Important clarification: it is not necessary at
all to be believers, follow a confession, or
have religious references in one's life to
appreciate the revelation of "non-duality."
This is not regulated by a God, be it punitive
or benevolent. It doesn't need an "unmoved
mover," in some way sentient.
It can simply be considered as a truth that
Science cannot yet prove, but that doesn't
cease to exist.

Just like gravitational interaction, which existed long before the birth of Isaac Newton. And which would still have existed, even without him.

Once we learn that we are therefore a fragment of the One, and that our existence is not limited to a few decades spent between ephemeral pleasures and human sufferings, the whole picture changes.
Our life is comparable to a movie or a comedy lasting a couple of hours: we watch it, perhaps we appreciate it or not, but when the curtain falls, we return home, to life "after the movie."
And certainly, the plot or screenplay of the movie will not be fundamental in our life.
Similarly, the events of the physical body (and its deceptive mind) do not affect the great miracle of life that we are, and always will be.
Because we were never truly born, nor will we ever truly die.

So why anguish over some fleeting misadventure?

Even without wanting to embark on an ascetic or meditative path, simply becoming aware of the above can really facilitate the process of overcoming episodes of stress, anxiety, and panic.

It will be enough to even just put into practice some yoga techniques: the one that follows, for example.

Controlled breathing

The most suitable key to regain control during a panic attack is undoubtedly to manage breathing. Excessive breathing, or hyperventilation, increases the severity of a panic attack. It is both a symptom and a cause of panic attacks, so it must be addressed as such.

I found that focusing on the breath, inhaling deeply and slowly, proved to be a practical solution for my panic attacks.

Based on an ancient *mantra* - a Hindu formula to be recited aloud or silently, or even just mentally - called *Hong-So*, we inhale thinking "Hong," and exhale thinking "So."

With eyes closed or half-closed, and with focus directed at the center of the eyebrows (the point called *Kutastha*, or "third eye"), we can take all the needed time, usually for more than a few minutes.

It is essential to understand how hyperventilation provides too much oxygen. Since it enters rapidly, the body does not have enough carbon dioxide to neutralize it. Consequently, the body cannot use it fully, making you feel short of breath.

If you feel dizzy, confused, or have vertigo during a panic attack, or have shortness of breath and numbness in the extremities, with a compressed chest and pounding heart, know that you were "hyperventilating." You might also have sweaty hands, dry tongue, and the sensation of cold sweat. You might shiver and feel weak.

The problem is therefore resolved by breathing evenly and regularly.

Panic attacks affect a wide range of people in all walks of life. But print it once again in bold: they are not a life sentence, and they can and should be treated. Learning to manage the onset of a panic attack can help to set you free, and to regain control.

XII.

FINALLY FREE

Congratulations, you've made it this far. It means you're truly on the right path to eliminating panic attacks once and for all. You're consciously starting this process with determination, so you're definitely gaining the right self-esteem along the way.

Of course, professional assistance and medicine are helpful, very helpful indeed. But nothing will ever be as effective as your willpower and dedication.

So, here are some final recommendations:

The web isn't always a friend
Now that you've started taking good care of yourselves and your condition, it's natural that you're seeking information everywhere, starting from this volume to more professional and specific literature.

The internet and books are an enormous source of information, but beware: learn to recognize, if you can, correct information from incorrect, reliable sources from less serious or unreliable ones.
In essence: gather information as much as you can, but always evaluate the source you're drawing from.

It will certainly do you good to know – and see it confirmed in various texts and websites – that anxiety, panic disorders, fight-or-flight responses are the result of a very natural chemical process (and more, as we've seen). Above all, it will help you avoid feeling like there's something wrong with you that's unsolvable or strange.

Cut down on stimulants
We've already discussed the effects of alcohol, coffee, and sugar on those suffering from panic attacks. Smoking is also known to

exacerbate panic attack symptoms by limiting blood flow and increasing adrenaline levels. Avoiding these elements will prevent them from disrupting the chemical balance in your brain.

Always check if the medications you're taking include stimulants. Even cold and flu medications, as well as some dietary supplements, may contain appreciable amounts of stimulants, potentially triggering a panic attack.

Yoga is a panacea

Yoga not only shapes and strengthens the body but also forces you to focus on relaxation and overall awareness of the body and mind. Massage and meditation also help relax muscles and minimize the tension that can easily build up before a panic attack. Try to allow yourself some relaxation time every day, make it a regular part of your routine. Your body and mind will thank you for it.

Inhale and exhale

Learning some effective breathing techniques might help reduce the well-known disturbances caused by hyperventilation. The worst elements of a panic attack are generally dizziness and chest tightness, as you fear your heart might stop or you might faint. Deep, slow breathing can help alleviate panic attacks. It can also help you focus on your breath instead of the things running through your mind. It allows you to ride the waves of terror and regain control of yourself.

I'm certain – and I say this from personal experience, not based on others' stories – that your desire to free yourselves once and for all from the unpleasant feelings of stress, anxiety, and panic will be stronger than the causes that trigger them. But you must believe intensely. I'll be there, ideally, cheering for you. I wish you a "Good life," free from anxiety and panic. Wholeheartedly.

"Anxiety and panic, they come and go
With time and patience, they'll start to slow
Breath deep and focus on the here and now
Let go of fear, let go of doubt

Find strength in self and those around
You are not alone, you are safe and sound
Recovery is a journey, a day by day fight
But with time, you'll find peace and light"